The Mee Street Chronicles:
Straight Up Stories of a Black Woman's Life

The Mee Street Chronicles:
Straight Up Stories of a Black Woman's Life

By Frankie Lennon

With an Introduction by Nikki Giovanni

The Mee Street Chronicles: Straight Up Stories of a Black Woman's Life

Published by
Kerlak Enterprises, Inc.
Kerlak Publishing
Memphis, TN
www.kerlak.com

ISBN: 0-9788777-4-8
ISBN 13: 978-0-9788777-4-3
Library of Congress Control Number: 2007921619
First Printing: 2007

Special thanks to everyone at Kerlak Publishing for all the encouragement and assistance.

This book is printed on acid free paper.

Printed in the United States of America

Contents

Part One: Mee Street Is Memory

Part Two: Baptism

Part Three: Tribes

To my parents, Mary Estelle & Coach George "Dusty" Lennon.

To all of the Lennon family.

To Knoxville and days gone by.

Acknowledgements

Thank you to Kaseema Jernigan, John Meeks, and Bishop Carl Bean who saw something in my writing when I couldn't. Thank you for believing in me enough to cheer me on from the beginning of this book to its end.

Thank you to Jair whose support and feedback has been instrumental in helping me shape the stories I tell in this book. You have been my editor and my cheerleader. Thank you for generously sharing yourself and your experience as a poet and writer with me. Without your insight, "Predators" might not be the story that it is.

Thank you to Ron Glass who told me back in 1980 when I was deeply depressed, afraid, and had given up on ever writing again:"just keep writing." Your words brought me back from the brink. "Baptism" is the story that you helped birth.

Thank you to Hedgebrook, a Women Writer's Residency, for giving me time in the summer of 2005 and Waterfall Cabin on Whidbey Island to write. Sharing time at Hedgebrook with the other women writers present, Titi, Donna, Angie, and Diana, led me to gather the courage to write "Scotch on the Rocks" and "Skirmishes." These stories would not exist without your nudging me to do them.

Thank you to my friend, and alter ego, Nikki Giovanni who started all this by asking me to write something for a book she was editing. That was when "The Code" was born. And that story kicked off the whole enterprise of my writing more stories about my life.

Thank you to all those writers and artists who gave me encouragement, who listened and gave me valuable suggestions. The list includes Joan Johnson, Tom Patchell, The Talking Drum participants, the Los Angeles Alumni of Hedgebrook, and members of The Soulful Salon.

For years of love and laughter, thank you to the people of: The Village Green Group, Back to Basics, Unity Fellowship of Christ Church, Los Angeles, the staff and volunteers of Minority AIDS Project from 1987-1997; and thank you to Kellii Trombacco, Valerie Spencer, Maria Lyons, Mark Forte, and Sande Harte.

And a last thank you to my Knoxville family for loving me for who I am. Special acknowledgments to: Janice and Calvin, Avon and Sheryl, Rosalyn and Clifford, Brenda, Nancy, Charlene, Sharon, and, posthumously, to Judy.

A Friendship - Introduction

Growing up in a small town is both good and bad. Good because you learn to work the crowd, play the game, skip-to-my-lou, as it were. You learn that people lie and their lies don't matter. You also learn folk tell the truth but truth doesn't change anything. And if you're attentive you learn that the only things that matter are who loves you...and who doesn't. Not why you are loved, nor did you deserve it, but only that you are loved.

We grew up in a small town, Knoxville, Tennessee. There are photographs of Frankie and me at her Aunt Helen's. We are cigarette girls. We have on pink, little tutu dresses. We looked sweet. In those days, when people still smoked, the host and hostess would buy a carton of cigarettes and open them. Frankie and I would walk through the grounds at the lawn party, or the house when it was winter, offering cigarettes to the guests. It was a pretty cool thing to do. Grandmother and I would walk from Mulvaney Street to Dandridge Avenue. She couldn't drive and I was too young. We didn't have a car either though I must point out we used to have a car. A Plymouth, black, two door. The salesman drove it to our door. But Grandmother never could learn to drive and I was too young. The salesman came and took it back. Grandmother's money was returned. We walked.

This is what I first remember: I was sitting in the Gem Theater getting ready to see a movie I have already forgotten. Frankie and five or six other girls came in. She was the leader of the group. They sat behind me. Frankie recognized me. She said to another girl. "That's Nikki, Ms. Watson's granddaughter. Should we ask her to sit with us?" Everybody said some form of "Yeah" or "Okay" and they asked me if I wanted to sit with them. I didn't.

What I remembered was that Frankie and I went way further back than that. Our mothers were both members of Delta Sigma Theta Sorority. Our fathers both chased the dreams men chase when they marry the women of their dreams. Frankie was a privileged Black American. She had the house, the car, the money, the church named after her family. Instead of at home in Cincinnati, I was in Knoxville because my parents fought, and I couldn't make any sense out of it. I was hoping my grandmother would let me live with her, and if she said no, I didn't know what I was going to do. No. I did not want to sit with Frankie and her friends in a segregated movie house. I wanted to find a way out of my nightmare.

Grandmother understood way more than I thought and I enrolled in school. I wish I had understood I was not the only person in pain during those teenaged years. I wish I had understood I was not the only person looking for someone to love. I got lucky. My mother's friends reached out; my teachers, Miss Delaney and Ms. Stokes, reached out; and, most especially, the librarian, Miss Brooks, reached out and I somehow held on. I went one morning to the Bijou Theater to see *Gog and Magog* which was not all that good a movie, but I had walked up to the front to get my ticket. I was, of course, sent to the back where I climbed the steps to watch Richard Egan in a science fiction movie. It wasn't so much the backstairs as the sort of smirk on the ticket-taker's face. That was my last movie for an awfully long time.

Frankie and the gang went to camp and Grandmother sent me to camp with them. They put a frog in my bed at which everybody laughed but me. I smothered the frog and I did not like killing it. Had I known, I would have stripped the bed. Everybody could swim but me. I still can't swim. And the idea that camp was supposed to be fun still escapes me. I almost got kicked out, but having been already kicked out of the Brownies, camp was minor. I made it through camp, but that wasn't the last thing. I was kicked out of college, fired from my first job, and generally misunderstood, so, quite naturally, I became a writer.

In high school, Frankie wrote *Julie and the Beatniks*. Forty years later, I learned that I was Julie: I was the rebel. I never thought of myself like that. I was, to me, the girl who didn't make the cheerleading squad though I tried out. I was the girl who couldn't fast dance. I was the girl who watched. I was the girl outside.

Frankie has a story to tell. She negotiated a very narrow path; she walked the line. Every generation has its Zora Neale Hurston, its voice of truth and clarity. Frankie Lennon is finding her way to a generational truth. It is not always a happy or funny story. But it is another side of a fabulous generation that changed the world. We all should read what Frankie has to say.

Nikki Giovanni, Poet

Part One:
Mee Street Is Memory

Knoxville, Tennessee

What we remember from childhood we remember forever – permanent ghosts stamped, inked, imprinted, eternally seen.

Cynthia Ozick

I wrote these stories because I needed to remember – things, and people, and places. How it used to be.

Frankie Lennon

Memory:
Mee Street and Beyond

"The root of oppression is the loss of memory."
Paula Gunn Allen, Native American writer

Knoxville, nestling in the bosom of the Great Smoky Mountains, which is part of the Appalachian mountain chain, was not a metropolitan area during the Truman and Eisenhower years when I was growing up; it was a mid-sized town, sitting on sloping ridges, steep grades, and rolling hills. Up and down, you were always going up and down in humpbacked Knoxville. And because ole Jim Crow reigned supreme, there were really two Knoxvilles—one White and one Black. I belonged to the Black side. Our first house, on Mee Street, was on the Black side of town and it stood directly across the street from the Austin Homes housing projects. I was an only child and I loved it there because my playmates were always just across the street at Austin Homes Projects, and when I wanted to play all I had to do was dash over there. Unfortunately, it was a very busy street, and I tended to do this dashing business without looking both ways for cars. As a result, I almost got myself mashed flat as a pancake, more than once. Watching me continue to run into the street without regard for life or limb, my mother finally threw up her hands, and convinced my father that we had to move to someplace with a big yard and no busy street. By the time I got to the second grade, we had moved to 1919 Dandridge Avenue, where we became the third Black

3

family to move into this middle class, previously lily-white neighborhood.

At first, the only other Blacks living there were my uncle Frank and his wife, Helen, whose only son had died several years before, and there were the Delaneys, whose children were grown. So in one fell swoop, I had gone from living in a place where I was surrounded by playmates and familiar Black faces to living in a place where I was the only kid around, surrounded by a sea of White folk whose intentions toward us were always suspicious. Mama strictly forbade me to leave the yard unless I was going to the little neighborhood store for her, or to Uncle Frank's, or to Mrs. Delaney's. For company, since I was now without Evelyne, Shirley, and my other playmates, my parents got me a fat, little white, black, and brown puppy—part Cocker Spaniel and part Bird Dog—that I named Pudgy.

Our new, white frame, two-bedroom house sat in the middle of huge front and back yards—way too big for one kid and one dog. The yards were so big that one summer my mother volunteered our place to host our church's two-week Vacation Bible School since there was enough room to comfortably accommodate a hundred scampering children. The one thing I liked about the yards was the flowers. I was obsessed with flowers—the scent, but, most of all, the colors. At Mee Street, we didn't have any, but here, things were different. Some flowers were already waiting their turn to peek out of the ground; others, Mama planted herself. I was always putting my nose into the heart of a flower, trying to sniff its nectar, or, sometimes, sticking my tongue into its heart to taste it as I had seen the hummingbirds doing. Mama taught me about the flowers, pointing to each as she said their names: pink peony, red zinnia, white crocus, yellow marigold, white pansy, blue snowballs, and purple iris. For some

4

reason, we didn't have roses. I don't remember why. But I'm sure I asked Mama about it because roses were my very favorites.

In spring, the mimosa trees, which dominated the front yard, presented rose-colored, spiky blossoms, framed by fringed, green leaves. I especially loved the mimosas because I had taken up tree climbing, and the mimosas were my favorite trees to climb. By Easter time, rows and rows of yellow daffodils and white jonquils nodding their delicate little heads in the morning breeze dominated one side of the front yard. While in the back yard, the trees—dogwood, Japanese tulip, pear and lime—offered up blossoms that looked like white and pink lace, or rose and crimson brocade. Banks of white honeysuckle, along the driveway, tickled and tantalized my nose with their sweet scents from April through August.

Summers are a memory: The delight of getting to go barefoot everyday and wiggle my toes in warm grass; racing Pudgy to the corner grocery store; discovering a blackberry patch one afternoon where I popped tart, plump berries into my mouth, while keeping a sharp eye out for snakes; catching fireflies in a jar at dusk and trying to figure out how their tails lit up; watching sweat run down Mama's cheek as she canned pear preserves from the tree outside; listening to the sounds of baseball games blasting on the portable radio, while Daddy, in Bermuda shorts and sleeveless undershirt, painted the house.

In a neighborhood where there were no other children, I became something of a loner, finding things to do in solitary—a characteristic of mine that abides to this day. Eventually, after Black folks moved in and the White folks moved out, I was allowed to roam freely. I would explore every nook and cranny I could find in the neighborhood. If there had been caves, I would have wandered in. I often wished there were. Caves sounded like a fine, high adventure and I liked adventure.

Which is why, I suppose, I liked to read fairy tales so much; they were full of adventure. I got so I could recite certain ones from memory, like *Rapunzel, Rumplestilskin, Snow White and Rose Red.*

Sometimes when my mother went uptown to bank and pay bills, she'd take me to the Colored public library branch where we could go in to read or check out books. Mama and I would have to ride the back of the city bus, and exit by the back door, but it was worth it to get to go to the library—the only one in Knoxville for Colored folks. Mama would ask the Black librarian to watch out for me, and she would leave, knowing I was in good hands. I never watched the clock or got impatient to go home because once there, I would go row by row, stack by stack, to find my beloved fairy tale stories. Eventually, I read every one in the library.

Back then, there weren't any children's books written for us—no stories in print so I could read about my gutsy and steadfast Black female ancestors: Women like Harriet Tubman, Sojourner Truth, and Ida B. Wells. No stories I could read to learn good things about myself. What little I did learn about Black people came from my fourth grade teacher, Mrs. Paul. Because she was a different kind of teacher who talked about the great things Black people had done and would do, her students thought she was an eccentric. We said she was: touched in the head, not all there, crazy as a bedbug. She wore her hair in a natural, pinned in a bun at the back of her neck, before anyone else had the nerve to do it. It was Mrs. Paul who taught us about Black History Week, and about Black writers like Paul Lawrence Dunbar and Phyllis Wheatley. She kept after us, saying: *Stand tall and be proud of who you are.* Mrs. Paul was ahead of her time in that way. I don't

6

remember any of my other elementary school teachers ever mentioning a mumbling word about our Black culture, writers, or history. I guess they were afraid for their jobs. Mrs. Paul said we'd remember her and what she'd taught us one day. Said she was leaving her mark on us. She was right. I do remember her. And she did leave her mark. I find myself saying the same sorts of things to my students that she said to us.

People need to remember things. Because memories tell a story. Memories mark who you are. The Knoxville I tell of here is no longer around. Yet it lives in my remembering. It lives in my stories. It lives because I need to remember, to tell the good and not so good of growing up in Knoxville. It lives because remembering tells me, and you, the story of who I am.

The Alcoa House

During the Jim Crow era, the rule of the day for Black folks boiled down to separate and unequal housing, schools, sports, jobs, salaries, opportunities, and a myriad of other things. In Knoxville, Daddy coached the boys' basketball team at Austin High and Mama, the girls' team. In Tennessee, segregation didn't allow White teams to play Black teams, and since Knoxville had only one Black high school, Austin's team had to travel out of town, and, sometimes, out of the state to play other Black teams in the Negro High School Athletic Association. Which meant my parents often had to go, as well. We were still living on Mee Street then, and I was between the ages of three and five, so when Mama and Daddy had to go overnight, Mama would take me to her sister in Alcoa to stay over. And, boy, did I dread those times when Auntie babysat me.

Auntie was already an old woman—in late her sixties, perhaps already seventy when I was born. Her birth year, I estimate, must have been somewhere between 1874 and 1884, around the time that the post-Civil War Reconstruction Era was aborted by greedy, northern White politicians and embittered southern Whites. I'm guessing that she was born and raised in the South although I'm not sure because folks in my family didn't talk much about the past. And Auntie didn't talk at all.

Not much to Mama. And, unless she had to, not at all to Daddy. Or me.

The drive to Auntie's was about thirty to forty minutes from Knoxville on a twisty, two-lane highway that took you first to the Tyson-McGee Airport and then on to Alcoa, a little company town, sprouting up around the aluminum corporate giant. I imagine that I must have squirmed, maybe even whined, each time we got near the Alcoa house. I imagine that I was not above begging my mother to turn the car around, go back to Knoxville, and let me stay with Aunt Lil, one of her best friends. Of course, I knew that begging her would do no good, but I just hated being left at the Alcoa house, left there with Auntie to sink down into her silent waters.

The rental house that she inhabited was the first one on the left as you drove into the city limits. I say "inhabited" because it seems so fitting rather than "lived in" now that I look back. For there was no lived-in, intimate feeling to the house and its surroundings. Unlike other Black women of her generation, Auntie had planted no garden, flower or vegetable, on the grounds. Between the highway and the front porch of her house, there was a small patch of yard and, really, no sidewalk. Three or four steps without handrails brought you up to the front porch, which—like the wood frame house itself—was unremarkable. There was no porch swing, like the one at Grandmama's house where you could sit, and gently sway yourself to sleep in late afternoons. No a chair, nor blooms in a flowerpot graced the porch to invite a passing neighbor to stop, come sit, and talk a while. In fact, nothing had been placed here to welcome you.

As you entered from the front door, near darkness greeted you because the plain, roll-down shades at the windows were always drawn shut. She kept the shades closed, she told Mama, to keep in it cool in summer and trap the heat in winter. But I always wondered why there were no curtains hung. None at any of the windows. This, along with the silence that always greeted me, made the house feel grim and cold. Going in, our footsteps—Mama's and mine—would tap a staccato beat against the bare floor, disrespectfully breaking the tomblike stillness. Mama would move forward purposefully, and I'd stop and squint in the dim light, looking around at the space of the living room that flowed into the dining room, looking for some place I could fit, somewhere I could be without feeling the intruder. I could never find it.

Mama would stride straight through the house into the kitchen which was back of the dining room. It was the one room Auntie kept to more than any other. I remember her standing in her always scrubbed and polished kitchen, the one place in the house where there were no shades and sunlight would sometimes shine into the windows. As usual, she'd be at the sink, her slight body stooped with age, and she'd be wearing a faded, blue housedress with a white, pinafore apron pinned to it, her feet clad in sturdy, black shoes, slightly run over at the heels, her legs swaddled in thick, beige, opaque stockings. Her shrunken, wrinkled face, framed by cotton-ball, white hair, was the color of blackberries, and dangling from her ears was the only jewelry she ever wore—a pair of small, gold, hoop earrings.

Standing back and away from wherever in the house Auntie happened to be, I'd hear Mama's soft voice reciting how long she and Daddy would be gone, and when they'd be back to pick me up. At the end, Mama would give me a peck on the cheek and a hug before disappearing out the front door. When the door clicked shut, Auntie would glance over at me, say nothing, and turn back to her work. A soundless veil would descend on the house, then as I found a corner at the kitchen table to sit. And wait.

I'd watch her in the kitchen, fixing dinner, washing and rinsing her favorite greens—mustard and turnip—to which she would add a bit of fat back for seasoning. My mouth would water at the sugary smell of sweet potatoes baking in their juices, and at the smell of stewing chicken just beginning to bubble on the stove in the beat-up, aluminum pot she always used. Like her house, her meals were plain, without much seasoning, but very good. She had a habit of drinking the peppery-spiced pot-likker, the leftover juices from cooked greens, a practice that I took up when I was with her. We ate our meals, silently, at the white, enameled, kitchen table. Afterwards, she would immediately wash and dry the dishes, put them away, then wipe the table and counters until they fairly sparkled. Her final task would be sweeping and mopping the floor. If sunlight flooded through the kitchen windows, it would fall, I remember, like liquid gold, on the scrubbed, now-spotless linoleum.

Why we never ate in the dining room, I don't know. There was a wooden table there, unadorned. It wasn't a table set to welcome guests—or anyone else—to dinner. No fruit bowl, no tablecloth was on it. No cushions lent comfort to the hard, wooden chairs set firmly at four places. The only person I remember ever sitting at the dining room table was my mother. She would use it as a desk to write a shopping list for Auntie. Her dining room was like her: austere, cold and erect. No scattered rugs were laid for color and warmth. The floors were just as bare as the pine-paneled, built-in bookshelves. For Auntie kept no books about the house. I never saw her—not even once—reading a book or a magazine or a newspaper.

Auntie was a woman who kept a house without frills or fancies. Nothing in it revealed or reflected anything about her. All of the walls in the house were bare except for the one just above the living room couch where Auntie had placed a calendar of landscapes. Because there was nothing for me to do, for Auntie allowed me no toy in her neat, dust-free living room, this one bit of "decoration" riveted my attention. Afraid to move, and forbidden to make noise, I would sit very still, gazing at the calendar pictures for what seemed like hours while Auntie cleaned or dusted or mopped. The calendar scenes replicated paintings of gloomy, cloud-shrouded mountains above soundless, dark glades, sunless forests, and rippling streams. They appealed to me, these pictures, because the painters had found some way to weave light into the shadows, to spin a glimmer of brightness within the shades of darkness. The dark in the pictures seemed to be made darker still by the snatches of light reflecting from the painted sky. In any case, they reminded me of Auntie's house: sad, dark, and soundless.

More than anything else, it is the absence of sound that haunts my memories of the Alcoa house. Auntie was a silent woman, one who rarely smiled. I can't remember us ever holding an everyday conversation. I don't even remember the sound of Auntie's voice, so I suppose that's a memory file I've deliberately deleted. But I know that Auntie hummed old hymns. That she sang snatches of the ones she loved, like "The Old, Rugged Cross" and "What a Friend We Have in Jesus," songs that I loathe to hear today for they remind me of her. Nevertheless, silence is what I remember when I think of the Alcoa house. The color of silence shrouds all of my memory.

There was no television then, and even if there had been, she would not have allowed one in her house. It would have been labeled as one of "the devil's works" and banned without a second thought. She had a radio, but not for the daily soaps, or weekly entertainment shows, and, certainly, not to play music. Those, too, were things of the devil, to her way of thinking. No, she only turned the radio on to hear the Southern Baptist church services she loved.

In her rocking chair, with *The Bible* open on her lap, Auntie mumbled "Amen," wept copiously, and sang along with the ranting, raving, southern, White, radio preachers. Preachers with an Appalachian twang in their voices exhorting you, commanding you to "Come to Jee-suz!" The kind that called you a sinner at least a hundred times in thirty minutes flat. The kind I grew to absolutely hate listening to. They never preached kindness or unconditional love. No. Charity was not on their collective minds. And that seemed to be just fine with Auntie. For she was, I much later came to understand, not a woman of charity, but one of religiosity and she wore hers proudly, like another woman would wear a full-length, mink coat.

That pride extended to the way she kept her house. Auntie had a horror—a positive phobia, about anyone ruining its spit and polish order. Especially her bedroom. Everything in the room was functional, and swept clean. The floors dared not show traces of dust. Cobwebs in ceiling corners were forbidden. The bed was made up with crisp corners and tucks. In that room, you'd find no mementoes or photos on the chest of drawers. Not even a doily, that lacy bit of cloth used as furniture decoration, was laid atop the dressing table.

Once, I made the mistake of sitting on her perfectly-made bed. Not just sitting, mind you, but bouncing up and down, humming some tune stuck in my head. With each bounce, the wrinkle-free, crisp, white bedspread was transformed into disorder. When she came out of the bathroom and discovered my offense, her face changed— no, not changed—contorted into a mask of fury.

"Never," she screamed, "sit on the bed when it's made up!"

I shrank back, paralyzed at the sound of the hysterical shrieks rolling out of her mouth.

As she jerked me off the bed, she continued her roaring tirade. "Beds are for sleeping! Sleeping, not sitting! Do you understand me, girl?"

In terror and confusion, I nodded that I did. For, at that moment, I would've agreed to anything to shut up this harpy, dancing with rage. I don't remember how long she went on, but when she finished, I was so thoroughly frightened that from then on, I never again approached the bed until she motioned for me to get into it at night.

After that, it was clear to me that Auntie barely tolerated my moving about in her house. Since she didn't want me underfoot inside, I tried to spend a lot of time outside. I can't really say I played out there because there was no one to play with. It was more like drifting from spot to spot in the back yard, then on to the front.

Finding something to hold my interest in the back yard wasn't easy. The yard was barren, strangely silent, and unlovely. Dry, dusty blades of grass clung desperately to the earth. It was a torture to be out there because I was a child who loved flowers and color, trees to climb, places to explore; and there were none. Nothing to climb. No hidden places where you could uncover delicious secrets. Nothing was out there except for two things: A small, wooden shed and a tall, wooden fence, too high for me to see over, which ran the perimeter of the yard. The shed was a dilapidated, gray thing with missing slats and trailing green vines climbing atop its roof. I remember that I was a bit afraid of the shed. I once peeped inside the door, which only opened part way, and saw what seemed like thousands of spider's webs, silvery and gleaming in the dark shadows. There was a musty, shut-up odor to it, a smell like rotting papers and old wood. Since I was afraid of spiders and not too fond of shut-up, dark places, I dared not go in. Instead, I would sit in front of it, staring at its sagging frame, thinking up scary stories to entertain myself about what was inside.

Finally, before day was done, I'd gravitate to the front yard where a few spindly shrubs stood here and there, plainly thirsty for love and water as was the threadbare grass, struggling to stay alive. At the tail end of the afternoon, I'd stand listening, in gathering shadows, to the high-pitched singing of evening cicadas. Feeling lonely and lost, the cricket sounds loud in my ears, I'd watch the cars whooshing by on Alcoa Highway.

To amuse myself, first, I'd imagine the people inside the cars were going somewhere special. Going to a place where there'd be light and laughter. Going somewhere far away from the dark Alcoa house. Then I'd begin to wait. And hope. Telling myself my parents might come sooner than they'd said. Might come today instead of tomorrow. Might come in a few minutes to take me away from this house—so mute, so still and solemn as a grave.

While afternoon turned to dusk, I'd be standing at the edge of the front yard, squinting to peer down the highway, wishing I would see Daddy's car drawing nearer, slowing down, and turning into the driveway. I'd be standing there, feeling a hollow place in my chest, wishing really hard that I'd see Daddy's car coming. I'd cross my fingers, then my arms, then my legs, and I'd say to myself over and over like a mantra: *They're coming for me soon. Coming for me soon. Coming for me soon.* I'd say the words as the sting of tears nipped at my eyes. Say them, believing that Mama and Daddy were in the car coming. Believing the car was just around the bend of the highway. The hollow place would press harder against my chest as I'd stand, chanting the words that I had to believe. Waiting there, beside the Alcoa house with darkness coming and silence creeping round me like a grave.

No Escape

1. Through the Witch's Forest

Night. I wake suddenly in my room. Not groggy, but wide-awake. And alert. My Cinderella table lamp is on, casting a pool of light near my bedside; the rest of the room is in shadows. The house feels wrong. Too quiet. Daddy's radio isn't playing in the living room, like always. Sitting up in my bed, I throw back the covers and scoot, so that my feet and stubby legs dangle over the side.

I call out: "Mama? Daddy?"

Instead of their voices, I hear my own echoing back to me. It's a creepy sound and I don't like it. To make myself feel better, I look to my left, toward the corner where my faithful horse, Trigger, is corralled. But my rocking horse is lost in shadows and the darkness shrouding it seems to stir. That frightens me, so I slide off the bed to the green rug covering the wooden floor, and go quickly on tiptoe to the door that connects to my parents' bedroom.

Once more, I call in a trembling voice: "Mama? Daddy?"

Silence answers me. It slithers through their bedroom. In the distance, I hear a clap of thunder. A shiver runs across my shoulders, and I want to go back and put my head under the covers, but I don't because I think there may be something hiding behind Trigger—something shadowy and hungry with huge, blind, groping tentacles.

No, getting back into bed alone is too scary. Besides, I want to find my mama and daddy.

So I wade into the liquid darkness of my parents' bedroom. Floorboards creek as I go. Because my eyes haven't started to adjust, I can't see in the inky blackness. Waving my arms around, I try to feel for some familiar piece of furniture, but there's nothing near save the darkness that embraces me with treacherous, black satin arms.

Somewhere in the house, I hear something thump. Lightning streaks and crackles through the sky, and, for a moment, the bedroom window is bathed in white light. Booming thunder crashes in the air just behind the lightning as darkness descends again. The rolling thunder sends little pricks tingling up my arms, and, suddenly, I feel like I can't breathe, can't move another inch. It's so dark. Maybe I could just sink to the floor, cover my head and go to sleep right here.

Except the voice of my godfairy mother whispers in my ear: *You can't stay here, Frankie. You must keep going. Be brave*, she tells me. *Remember Hansel and Gretel!*

The story of Hansel and Gretel is one of my favorites. They were lost, I remember, lost and stumbling through the witch's forest but Gretel was brave. She held her brother's hand tightly and kept taking step after step.

Be like Gretel! Says my godfairy mother.

Yes, I tell myself. I can pretend to be like her with my imaginary brother beside me in the dark. We can cross the witch's forest in the bedroom safely together. And I go forward once more, hurrying, this time, as best I can in the dark.

2. Land of the Shadow-things

Crossing the forest-bedroom seems to take forever.

Finally, though, I reach its edge and stand at the entrance to the living room. Outside, closer now, thunder explodes again. Radiant light flashes.

Softly, I say: "Daddy?" No one answers. The living room is so black that it shimmers in lightless gloom. Somewhere something thumps again, followed by a low humming. At the sounds, hot terror bites at my legs and I begin fumbling about the walls, trying to remember where the light switch is. I fumble and fumble but it's no use. I can't find the switch I've seen Daddy push because I am too little to reach light switches. From the corner of my eye, I think I see a shadow creeping toward me. Whimpering, I hug the wall and close my eyes. Some desperate feeling I have no name for roots me to the spot until my godfairy mother whispers to me again.

If you stay still, she says, *that's when the forest witch gets you. She swoops down on you when you can't move. She swoops down, puts you on her broom, takes you to her kitchen, and stuffs you in the oven to bake you like your Mama's Sunday chicken.*

That gets me moving. I know a hiding place if I can just get there. My big toe stretches out first, then my whole right foot slides out, and after that, I make three, big leaps across the room to the big wing chair. "Home free," I say to myself as soon as my fingers touch the chair's smooth fabric. I clutch at it, happy to be near something safe, something to protect me. This is where Daddy sits with me on his lap while we listen to *The Adventures of Sherlock Holmes* on the radio. After I scramble into the chair, I scrunch down and push my back into it, picturing Daddy in the chair with me, my head on his shoulder and his big, bear arms hugging me tightly. There's a table lamp just next to the chair, I remember. If I turn it on, the hungry shadows might disappear in the light. Slowly, I stand up, peep over the top of the chair's wing, and reach out to tug the lamp's pull chain. When I do, an arc of light magically appears.

"Mama?" I say loudly into the silence.

She doesn't answer. I look across the room at the black upright piano that she loves where I struggle daily to make pleasing sounds come from the keys. Silence vibrates in my ears. *Where are they?* I ask silently. My glance falls on the far corner where shadows seem to coil, twist, and dart out at me. I cover my eyes with both my hands and look away. A question comes slithering horribly into my head: *Did the monsters get my mama and daddy?* My godfairy mother gives me no answer. And the house stands mute.

Quickly, before the shadow-thing can get at me, I jump out of the chair and make a mad dash for the front door knob. It's almost too high for me to reach, but standing on tippy toes, I can just get my little fists around it. I twist hard. Pull it toward me. Twist again and again until I finally understand that it's locked. Now, I stretch upwards with my hand, but the lock is set into the door high above the knob. I cannot reach it. Panic sets in. A storm of tears swells up inside me, matching the rain that storms outside.

You're all by yourself, whispers an evil voice in my mind. *Bluebeard is waiting for you somewhere in the darkness, clutching a huge knife dripping with the blood of his beheaded wives.*

I quickly cover my eyes with my fingers.

There's no escape! Purrs the evil voice. *The forest witch is getting on her broomstick to come for you.*

Peeking through my fingers at the shadowy corners of the room, I sob quietly into my hands, feeling doomed and trapped.

No, not trapped, whispers my godfairy mother. *What about the kitchen door?*

Sniffing back my tears, I look toward the kitchen. Yes, I'd forgotten the back door in the kitchen.

But, the evil voice warns, *that would mean going through the darkness in the dining room where there are THINGS that will catch you in their slimy, writhing arms.*

Fright squeezes my bladder so hard I almost pee on myself as I squint up my eyes, looking hard into the darkened dining room. Although the scared part of me tells me not to go, I make myself ignore it and take the first step in that direction.

Carefully, I tiptoe to the entrance, holding my breath. Before I go in, I stop, trying to see into the gloom. Nothing moves. I slide in, my back hugging the wall, willing myself to be invisible to whatever is in there. Hardly breathing, I move toward the kitchen, hoping to see nothing, but ready to make a dash if I see any slimy things lunging at me. Halfway through, a black shape suddenly looms up out of the darkness. I feel something hard hit my forehead, dazing me for a moment. I freeze and as my eyes focus better, I see the shape of the big, mahogany buffet against the wall, and I realize I have stumbled right into it. Light is coming from the kitchen door just bright enough to show me the rest of the way and I make a run for it. Out of the corner of my eye, slimy shadow-arms snake out to catch me, but I'm too fast for them.

Inside the kitchen, I scramble for the back door and look up for the doorknob. When I see the door is latched, too far above my head for me to reach, my heart falls, and I begin to sob.

Locked in, the evil voice in my head cackles. *The shadow-things will get you soon because there's no escape!*

Terror presses into my chest. I am alone and the monsters are going to deal with me. Desperately, I wail: "Daddy, where are you? Mama, come and get me!!"

3. Flight

Outside, thunder rumbles and rain patters down hard, sounding like footsteps on the roof. I sob louder, knowing that any minute Bluebeard will come through the door to cut me up with his bloody knife, and then, the forest witch will bake me in her oven, and then, the giant will gobble me up for his Sunday dinner. I stumble across the kitchen and sink down, burying my wet face in my hands. Something nudges me, and I hear the so-soft whisper of my godfairy mother, but it's so low that I can't make out her words. Another nudge. I look behind me. It's the stepladder chair I'm sitting on that's poking me in my back.

This time, I hear when my godfairy mother says: *Push the stepladder chair up close to the door, so you'll be tall enough to open it.*

I jump up, and begin shoving the chair across the room. As I'm pushing, I think I hear a noise in another part of the house.

"Was that a scraping sound?" I say aloud.

I stop pushing and listen hard while bits and pieces of the Saturday afternoon movies that I adore flash across my mind: Was that the Mummy? I wonder. He makes a sound like that when he drags his foot on the floor. Or was it a thump? Like Dracula's coffin opening? Panic, barely contained, runs its fingers across my throat, and I feel a scream caught there, waiting to come out.

Instead of screaming, I give the stepladder chair a final push against the door and climb up. Now, I'm tall enough now to reach the latch, but it won't open even though I pull hard. As I pull and pull, I think I hear another sound. Like something creaking. I make myself ignore it, clamping my lips together hard so I won't make a sound, and I look at the latch that keeps the door shut. Raising the fingers of my right hand, I trace the shape of latch hook fastened to the loop. I remember seeing Mama open it, but I don't know how.

A noise. This time I know I hear a noise. Panic shoots through me, screaming: *SOMETHING IS COMING! GET OUT! SAVE YOURSELF!*

But godfairy mother tells me the only way to save myself is to push the scaredness away; that way, I can make myself remember how Mama undoes the latch. I picture her in my mind with her black hair tied back in a red scarf, undoing the hook to let me go outside into the Saturday morning sunshine. Then, I close my eyes while I let my fingers imitate Mama's fingers lifting the hook to take it out of the loop. I don't know how much time it takes, but all of a sudden, I can tell I've worked the hook free. I open my eyes and grab at the knob, pulling. Then, I hear the sound of wings flapping. Dracula's wings? The door opens only few inches. "Why won't it open?" I whisper in fear and frustration.

Then, I realize the chair I'm standing on is blocking the door. Quick as a flash, I jump down, push it away, and jerk the door until it swings all the way back. The rain has changed into light sprinkles and the air is sweetly fresh in my face. For just a moment, I hear flapping sounds again, coming closer; then, I leap over the threshold onto the back porch, hardly feeling the wetness of the wood on my bare feet, or the wind whistling through my nightgown. Flying down the porch steps and out into the night, I feel the hot breath of a shadow-monster just behind me.

As I run down the street toward Austin Homes Projects, I look back. Something dark flaps and flutters just behind me. I streak ahead of it, racing toward Mr. and Mrs. Hale's apartment. When I reach it, I let out a high scream and beat my little fists against their door.

"Hurry! Oh, hurry!" I babble. "It'll catch me here if you don't hurry!" Fear squeezes me so hard I stand there wetting myself.

Moments later, Mrs. Hale opens the door. "Heaven sakes, child," she says, leaning down to me, her salt and pepper hair covering her shoulders. "What're you doing here in the middle of the night?"

Mr. Hale is beside her in his robe. "Where are your parents?" He asks, looking out into the night. Then, he scoops me up, and takes me inside.

Safe, I say to myself. *The shadow-monster can't get at me now.*

He takes me into their living room and covers me with a soft, blue blanket. They bring me milk and a brownie to eat while they talk quietly to each other. Halfway through the brownie, I fall asleep.

Later, Mama's voice, like a soft wind, wafts through my sleep. I open my eyes to see first Daddy, then Mama bending over me; their faces are full of worry.

My godfairy mother whispers: *See, the shadow monsters didn't get them after all.*

I smile at that while Mama kisses my nose; Daddy picks me up and I put my arms around his neck. My eyes are heavy, but I can just make out Sandman in the distance. He's beckoning me.

Escape is hard work for a three-year old, he says, sprinkling sand from his big bag into my eyes. *Come and sleep here where there are no shadow-monsters.*

Skipping happily, I follow him through Lullaby Glen, which winds down and down and down to Sleepy Time Hollow. There, my godfairy mother sits me on a fluffy, cloud-pillow, and I gladly slip down inside its snuggly warmth. While she waves at me, I float away, smiling, to the Land of Nod where sweet dreams come to fill my head until morning.

Adversaries

1. High Noon

When I eased into the kitchen from the backdoor, Auntie was sitting at the table shucking corn. Her hair was white as the cotton apron she wore pinned to her faded, flowered housedress, and her gold earrings caught the line of afternoon sunlight coming through the windows. Their shine caught my eye and a few moments passed before I noticed she was giving me an evil look from under her hooded eyelids. The iris of her eyes were a light hazel and when she looked at me, it made me think of the pictures of wolves my kindergarten teacher had shown us. Whenever she looked at me with those eyes, I felt like she had it in for me, like she was going to do something bad to me. For the thousandth time today, I wished that Mama and Daddy hadn't gone out to Knoxville College for that meeting. I was four. Why did I have to have a babysitter? Especially Auntie.

"Little girl," she finally said, "where you been?" Her voice reminded me of the threatening, low growl that Mrs. Hale's dog, Butch, makes when the kids tease him.

I lowered my head, afraid to look directly at her. "Outside," I whispered, hand in my hair, twisting two of my plaits together.

She said nothing for a time. Just stared at me. I hated having to wait for her to start in on me about whatever she thought I'd done wrong; waiting made me feel twitchy, but I told myself to stay still while I watched for her next move.

She was mad at me. I knew that for sure. My playmate, Shirley, had told me why in that Mama-doll voice of hers. Auntie, she said, had been standing on the porch yelling for me to come home, and, all of a sudden, she'd rushed across the street to The Square. Which was the spot in the middle of Austin Homes Projects where all the neighborhood kids played. They'd scattered when they saw Auntie coming cause everybody could tell by the way she was walking that she was mad. Shirley hadn't moved fast enough, and Auntie had caught up with her. Auntie started shaking her like a rag doll, hollerin for Shirley to tell her quick where I was. Shirley told her she didn't know, cryin and tryin to get away from Auntie at the same time. Shirley said she was so scared she'd almost peed on herself. And that the only thing that saved her was her mama runnin out of the house to find out what was the matter. That's when she got away from Auntie and took off to look for me. Everybody at The Square knew I was scared of Auntie. For that matter, they were scared of her, too.

At the end of Shirley's story, Evelyne had said: "Uh, oh," tugged at her top plait, and looked around for Auntie, like she was figuring out which way to run if she had to.

Shirley had said in that dolly voice of hers: "She's really, really mad at you." Then she'd pushed her thumb into her mouth, like she always did when she was excited.

I didn't say a word, just dropped the jacks Evelyne had been tryin to teach me to play, and started home.

Now that I was here, what was Auntie gonna do? Wondering gave me the shakes. All I could do was wait and watch.

"Didn't you hear me callin you, girl?" Auntie's voice was rising like the summer heat while her wolfie-eyes were boring little holes into my skull.

I shook my head no. Because of the noise at The Square, I really didn't hear her. Like usual, The Screaming Meemies kept up a lot of racket on Saturday morning. That's why Daddy called us that.

Grunting, she pushed herself up from the kitchen table. "What's that you got there in yo hand, young un?" Auntie pointed at my hand with the ear of corn she was holding.

Looking down at my fist, I realized I was still clutching one of the marbles we used to play Jacks. I didn't want to show her because Auntie didn't hold with playin games. She said they were sinful idleness and a waste of time. I sighed. Seems like I couldn't do anything right for her. She made me feel like the taste of castor oil Mama had me take sometimes.

"Come here," she growled. "Lemme see what's in yo hand."

I went slowly, keeping some distance between us in case I had to run. Finally, I stuck my hand out and opened my fingers. The opaque blue of the marble gleamed in my dirty, dusty hand like a stolen jewel.

She spied it and I saw danger in her eyes. She took a step closer to me. "You been playing with marbles, have ya?"

I moved backwards from her, and, in spite of my fear, anger rose up in my mouth. I lifted my eyes and met hers. "Daddy lets me," I answered with a tad too much backbone.

Wrong answer. Her face changed and I knew I'd gone too far. "I ain't yo Daddy and I ain't having no sass from you!" As she shouted at me, spit flew from her mouth. "The Lord don't like a sassy-mouth child! Don't nobody like a sassy mouth! Ya better learn! They string yo black ass up for sassiness. Get outside right now and get me some switches. You need a lesson!"

I flew out of the door and down the back steps like a blue streak. As I went, she hollered: "And make sure you get good, strong ones. Don't bring me no little ones that's gonna break. Else I'll whup yo behind harder."

2. In the Backyard

Down in the backyard, I let out a big sigh, wondering how I'd managed to get on Auntie's bad side. I wasn't trying to. It was that mouth of mine. It had the habit of saying things grownups didn't like to hear. But what was wrong with games? I didn't understand. It was so unfair when grownups made rules you had to follow that didn't make sense. I was just trying to learn Jacks from Evelyne so the kids wouldn't make fun of me. And now look at what happened. Auntie was gonna give me a lickin.

Chills went up my back as I realized that Auntie had never whipped me. Not even the time I'd bounced up and down on her bed; she'd only screamed at me then, and, boy-oh-boy, that had been scary enough. Tears puddled in my eyes, and I sat down under a tree and bawled. Auntie musta heard me cause she shouted down: "Shut up that noise out there! You hear me? You don't want me to come down there! Shut up that cryin right now!"

But I didn't. Sobbing, I stumbled around in my back yard, breaking off tree branches for switches, and rubbing at the tears rolling down my cheeks. After a while, I wiped my wet, dusty hands on my blue overalls. My dirty hands left brown streaks on them. Looking down at myself, I frowned. I'd probably get in more trouble with her for getting my clothes dirty. Sighing, I pushed back the blue clothespins clamped to the ends of each of my tiny plaits;

they swarmed about my face like bees. Auntie fussed about so many things I did. Not like Grandmama.

Thinking about my grandmama made me cry again. I wished I was in Grandmama's kitchen now. Where it smelled of hot, buttery rolls and brownies baking in the oven. Where I could play and nobody fussed or frowned at me. Where Grandmama smiled, put her arms around me, kissed me, and whispered: *I love you.* Where was she?

In the box, my mind whispered. *She was in that box they closed up at church.*

No! I screamed back at my mind. *No, no, no!*

At that moment, a woman's voice rang out in song from the church next door to our house. I choked off a sob and looked across the empty lot that stood between our back yard and the one-room church, peeling and fading to gray. What she was singing was full of rainy day, sad notes. Like the song they'd sung at church the day Grandmama was in the box. I'd put that memory in a shutaway place I'd made in my mind, so I wouldn't have to think about it. I didn't want to now, but the song was letting hurt-bad memories leak out from the shutaway place. And I couldn't stop them.

Everybody was there at my church. Me, Mama, Daddy, Aunt Claire, Uncle Matt, Uncle Frank, Aunt Helen, Reverend Dykes, and the Sunday church people. But it wasn't Sunday. And why was a big box in front of the altar with white and red and yellow flowers all around? When I looked up at Daddy sitting beside me, his chocolate face was all covered with tears. That scared me cause I'd never seen tears on his face, and, then, I heard somebody else crying really loud, and I looked to my right, and saw my Uncle Matt with tears on his face, and that scared me, too, cause I love my Uncle Matt almost as much as Daddy. I frowned and looked up at Mama sitting on the other side of me, and I squeezed her hand real tight, wanting to ask why they were cryin, but something told me not to, and I kept quiet.

Then, pretty soon, people lined up like we do in kindergarten for lunch, but I didn't see any food to eat, just the church people passing by the box in front. And then we lined up and walked by the box, but I couldn't see what was in it until Mama lifted me in her arms, holding me up above it, and I looked down. Grandmama was in there all dressed up. But she didn't have her glasses on and her eyes were closed. She was asleep. But why was she asleep in a box at church?

So I asked: "Why is Grandmama sleeping in the box, Mama?"

And Mama said: "She's not sleeping, honey. Grandmama has gone away."

And I said: "Is she coming back, Mama?"

And Mama said: "No, honey, she's not."

But I knew Grandmama wouldn't just leave me. Why was she gone? Before I could ask, Mama started turning away, taking me away from Grandmama.

I stretched out my hand to reach her before she could go away. Because I didn't want her to go; I couldn't let her go. I reached back with all my might over Mama's shoulder. Then I opened my mouth and screamed and screamed: "No! Come back!" Mama kept walking, and I kept screaming: "No! No! Come back, come back, Grandmama!"

It hurt to remember. Hurt badder than when I scraped both my knees bloody. Badder than when somebody stole Silky, my cocker spaniel. I didn't want to feel anymore hurt in my chest, so I pushed the picture memories back into the shutaway place, locked it, and made myself think of magic spells. If I could make the right one, I would swoosh my magic wand, make Grandmama come back right now, and Auntie disappear. It was then that I suddenly remembered Evelyne telling me that she had overheard her mother saying that my grandmama had passed away. Evelyne had said she asked her mama where you passed to, and could you come back. Her mama didn't say anything about where; she just told Evelyne that you couldn't come back. This time, I sensed, magic spells wouldn't work. Loneliness made me lift my face to the sky. It was where Mama said Grandmama had gone. The sky was so big, so blue, so wide. Grandmama was lost in it somewhere. And I'd never find her again. Never see her again. The thought pierced my heart deep in its core.

3. Duel

I didn't want to go back inside to Auntie, but I couldn't see anyway not to, so I climbed the back steps, holding the branches I'd gathered behind me. At the top of the steps, I hesitated, and quietly peeped through the kitchen door screen. She was standing at the sink counter, humming one of her church songs, chopping up pieces of ham, and throwing them into the big, iron pot filled with greens. Glumly, I stared at dangling, gold hoops on her ears. For the rest of my life, I realized with a jolt, I was gonna be stuck with Auntie. Misery cut my heart into a million pieces and resentment made soup out of it.

As I stepped inside, she put the knife down, ran water from the faucet over her hands, and dried them. "Where's them switches I done sent you to get?" Auntie asked me.

Without speaking, I walked toward her, and held out the four branches I was clutching. She peered hard at them first, and then snatched them out of my hand. I moved away to sit down in a kitchen chair. There was silence as she slowly examined each branch. At first, I had tried to find little switches, the kind that wouldn't sting or leave whelps, but I chickened, afraid if I brought little branches back, she'd whip me all the harder. In the end, I had followed her orders. The branches were big ones, long, with the leaves still attached. I trembled to think how they'd sting when they touched my behind.

Satisfied that I'd done what she said, she nodded and started pulling the leaves off. "Yo mama and daddy spoils you. Don't know why yo mama spoils you. Prob'ly that daddy of yours leadin her. When I was raisin her, I didn't spoil ya mama. A child needs to learn the straight and narrow road early."

I hated the talking-to grownups always gave you before you got a whipping. Most times, I wanted to say something back. One or two times, I did, and found out that was a bad idea cause if you did, if you fussed with them, then the whipping was stretched out longer, and you got harder licks. So, I learned to keep my mouth shut.

"I did m'best raisin ya mama. I cain't be faulted for the way things was. I did my part, kept m'pledge to m'dyin mother, even though I lost a husband b'cause of it. " She stopped talking and made a face. "Lord, have mercy, these menfolk! They cain't be trusted to do right. None of em. I had me two husbands, so I knows what I be speakin on."

The leaves were gone and, now, she began stripping off the bark. I shivered. When you took the bark off, the switches stung you like crazy. Made the whipping hurt worse. I wanted to run out, but to where? And running away would mean double trouble cause I'd have to come back sooner or later. I felt trapped, like the bad guys in the movies who had to shoot their way out of a box canyon.

She glared at me with frozen eyes. "An them marbles you playin with! Sinful idleness! That's why you didn't come when I called you. Too busy playin with marbles!" Mouth turned down, she shook her head and the gold earrings flashed in the light. "Jus cause yo daddy lets you play them games, you think it's fine and dandy." Now, she was plaiting the stripped down switches together into one switch. "Humph! I'm warnin ya. Menfolk'll set yo feet on the path of sin, and then, Lord! Lord! They up an leave ya. Lord, have mercy! You know, Lord, I be speakin yo truth!"

When Auntie talked to God, it made me feel funny, like ants or something crawlin up my arm. She sounded crazy and it usually scared me, but her talking bad bout Mama and Daddy was making me mad. Made me forget to be still in the chair. I'd started swinging my feet back and forth. She noticed.

"Be still, there, you," she yelled, scrunching her face up. "Y'need to listen to what I'm sayin."

I stopped fidgeting like she said, but I knew that wouldn't please her. Even if I faked it and acted like I wanted to hear what she was saying, she wouldn't be pleased. Nothing I did ever pleased Auntie. If I only knew what she wanted, I'd try to do it so she wouldn't fuss and frown at me. The thing was I never knew what she wanted me to do; she didn't give me any hints. With her, it was like groping in the dark, so easy to lose my way or hit my knee.

"That daddy of yours—you think the sun rise and set in that daddy of yours, but you don't know im. You an yo sassy ways. Ya don't know what I know. Yo mama die, he ain't gonna be around. He'll leave ya high and dry. I know it's a fact that menfolk always be leavin."

What she said about Daddy scared me. My mind made a picture of Mama in one of those boxes like Grandmama, and me all by myself looking down at Mama in the box. The thought squeezed my insides hard, like one of those big, jungle snakes, and I couldn't get my breath.

"You think if yo mama die, somebody gon take you in?" A wintertime smile touched Auntie's mouth, but not her eyes. "You doted on yo grandmamma, but she done left this here world, and yo aunts and uncles ain't gonna take you cause you too big for your britches. You better pray to the Lord yo Mama don't leave this world cause if she do, you ain't gon have nobody to take care of ya." Her face lit up as she finished. Like she had won something. Or I had lost.

While I was thinking about what she'd said about Daddy, scary thoughts ran through my head. Auntie was being mean, but what if she was right? I'd be alone like when I got locked in the house by myself. Bad things almost got me that time. I felt my face getting hot as all my feelings boiled and bubbled inside and finally, I opened my mouth.

"No!" I shouted, jumping out of the chair. "Daddy loves me! He wouldn't leave me!" But despite my words, I was scared.

She looked me straight in the face. "Humph! Yo daddy be hightailin it outta here if yo mama die." She pointed a gnarled finger in my face. "An ain't nobody gonna want a sassy girl like you. I sho wouldn't want you. Yo head too hard."

That hurt my feelings. Bad. A rainstorm of tears twisted inside me, and out they came in a downpour. The stubborn part of me didn't want her to see me cry, but I couldn't help it. I wiped at the tears with the backs of my hands and boo-hooed.

"You shut up that cryin," she snapped.

I couldn't make myself stop even though I could see that crying was making her really mad. Which, I figured, would mean she'd whip me even harder. And I understood dimly that she'd already hurt me really badly inside with what she'd said about Daddy, so could her whipping on my backside be any worse?

"I'ma give you something to cry about. I'ma teach you a good, old-fashioned lesson."

With a shock, I realized that she had finished plaiting up the switches; a deep stab of fear went through me as she came closer and closer, lifting the braided switch high. I looked up at it, knowing it was going to sting and cut; automatically, I shrank back, trying to run away, but I was trapped. There was no place to go.

Something rose up in me then and before I had time to think about what I was doing, I reached out and grabbed the switch in midair. "No!" I shouted. "I'm not gonna let you whip me! No! You're mean and hateful!"

Shock and surprise stopped her, but after a few seconds, she recovered and jerked at the switch, trying to get it out of my hands. Once I had it, though, I wasn't about to let it go. We pulled on it back and forth until she saw that I wasn't going to let go of my end. Then, she stopped. We looked at each other in the hot, quiet morning with the switch, like a rope, stretched between us. We just stood there, holding on to the two ends, not saying a word to each other.

Later, I'd think that it was just like the big duel at high noon in the westerns with the good guy staring down the bad guy just before they drew their guns. Once, when we were at the movies, Daddy had explained the good guy and the bad one were ad-ver-somethings. Which meant they were enemies. And that's why they were fighting.

Down the street, I could hear Butch barking as Auntie finally said: "You got as much spunk as yo mama had when we took her in even though them peoples of hers tried to beat it outta her." She tilted her head and looked at me. Like she was looking at something she'd never noticed before.

I wondered what and wanted to ask her. But I didn't. Auntie went on talking, her voice full of something funny, her wolfie-eyes looking at some place far off. "I was grown, and courtin when my mama and daddy took her in. She was a little bit of a thang then, all black and blue and hurtin, but Esther had her some spunk. My Lord, didn't she have her some spunk?"

What was *spunk*? I wanted to ask. From the way Auntie's voice sounded, it seemed like something good. The far-off look on Auntie's face was going away and, now, she looked at me close. "Ya look like her. Look like that daddy of yorn, too. But right now, ya puts me in the mind of Esther when I first laid eyes on her."

Then, she was quiet. Something she remembered made her eyes go far away again. I wished I could see what she was seeing, wished I could see it out of her eyes. Maybe then, I would understand her. Maybe then, I would know how to please her.

When she spoke, her voice quivered. "Beat her pretty bad, them folks a hers did, but they didn't kill her spunk." Her eyes came back to me, then fixed on the switch. "You comes by it honest," she said. "I oughta whip yo behind. Oughta but I ain't. Least not today." And she let the switch go.

I gaped at it dangling in my hand. Why had she let go? I didn't know the answer to that. What should I do next? Run out before she could change her mind? Stay where I was? Say something? I didn't know that answer either. Before I could figure it out, she turned away from me, moved to the counter, and reached for the bag of corn meal standing near the mixing bowl.

Over her shoulder, she said: "You still too big for yo britches, so you stay in yo room til yo mama get back. Don't be tryin to go back outside no more today."

I kept standing there like the world's biggest dummy.

"Go on now!" She told me.

I dropped the switch and ran.

4. Puzzles

In my bedroom, I stared out of the open window at Austin Homes Projects, my mind whirling in a ball of confusion. It was really hot and the kids had deserted The Square. Mee Street was quiet. To give myself something to do, I tried to play with my United States puzzle, but none of the leftover pieces fit where I tried to put them. After that, I picked up the set of Jacks Daddy had bought for me. No good though. I couldn't make my fingers do right. On the floor next to my bed was the book Mama was reading to me. I picked it up and turned the pages, staring at the pictures of Cinderella, the pumpkin, the fairy godmother, but nothing could keep my attention cause my head kept asking questions that I didn't have answers for. Like why did Auntie let me go without whipping me? And what was all that about Mama she was saying? Something about spunk, whatever that was. And who was it that beat Mama?

Too many questions. They made my head hurt, so I lay down on my yellow bedspread, and fell asleep for most of the afternoon. Later, I woke up wondering what Mama would say and do when Auntie told her that I'd dared her to whip me, and then grabbed the switch. Sitting up on my bed, I asked myself if I had ever done anything this bad before? I thought about it. Was this as bad as the time I took the jar of raspberry jam out of the refrigerator and ate the whole thing? Mama made me go without ice cream treats for five days for that one. Was this worse than the time I snuck over and stole the red rose from our next-door neighbor's yard? Mama whipped me and wouldn't let me go over to The Square for a week. I cried a lot over that one because I could see Evelyne and Shirley and the other kids from my bedroom window having a good time without me. That was bad. As bad as the time Mama said

I couldn't listen to my favorite radio mystery shows, *Mr. and Mrs. North*, *The Shadow*, and *Inner Sanctum* for two weeks, or go with Daddy to the Saturday movies I loved, all because I'd talked back to Mrs. Hill, my kindergarten teacher. I guessed this was worse than those other things. Way worse. So what was Mama gonna do to me for this? Thinking about it made me shake in my shoes.

Just then, I heard Daddy's voice as he and Mama got out of the car in front of the house. A lump of fear stuck in my throat as I tried to swallow. The thought of Mama's giving me a "hard lesson," as she called it, made me feel like I'd swallowed a frog and he was jumping around inside my belly. I remembered what she'd said this morning: "I'm depending on you to be a good girl and mind Sister. You know she's old and kind of peculiar." Daddy had looked funny when Mama had said that. Like he was mad or something. And Mama had asked: "Can I depend on you, Tiddley?" Tiddley was her special name for me. I'd said she could. But things had turned out so I couldn't keep my promise.

I heard Mama call to Auntie when she was coming in the front door. I could hear Mama and Auntie talking, but their voices weren't loud enough for me to understand what they were saying. Soon enough, Mama, in her new, candy-apple red suit, came to my room. "Come on, Tiddley," she said, "shake a leg. Sister's bus leaves in thirty minutes, and we have to take her to the bus station."

Slowly, I wiggled off the bed and stood. Mama walked over to my little white dressing table, and picked up my hairbrush. Uh, oh. I was gonna get it now. She was gonna use the hairbrush to whip me. I didn't move, or try to run. I just stood there waiting for the first lick, sure that Auntie had told on me. Instead of Mama tearing into me good, she came over, sat me down, brushed and plaited strands of hair that had got loose while I slept. After she finished, she hurried me out into the living room.

As I trotted along beside her, I told myself that she was gonna give me what-for in the living room with Auntie egging her on, and Daddy looking sad like he usually did when I got a whipping. The thought slowed me down a little, but Mama put her hand on my back and pushed me forward. In the living room, first thing I saw was Auntie sitting on the couch, dressed in her gray, Sunday outfit, her housedress and apron packed in a Miller's shopping bag at her feet. I couldn't tell about Auntie's feelings from her face. Seemed like it was closed tight as the pocketbook she had under her arm. Those eyes of hers iced up when she saw me looking her way, and I was sure she'd already told Mama. Out of the corner of my eyes, I saw Daddy with that funny, mad look he always had on his Hershey bar face when Auntie was around; he was squirming in his favorite chair, the one with the lamp beside it. Any second, I was sure to catch it. I peeked at Mama to see if she had the hairbrush in her hand; it surprised me that she didn't. Well, maybe she was gonna ask me to explain myself first. Sometimes, she did that before she gave me a whipping. Then she'd go get the belt or the hairbrush.

Funny. Nobody said anything though until Mama said: "Let's go. Frankie, you and Coach go on down first. I'll help Sister."

And we all went outside to the front steps. Daddy went ahead of me, but I hesitated, confused. Why wasn't Mama fussing at me for what I did? Why wasn't I getting a whipping? I glanced at Auntie again. Looked like she was staring daggers at me. I opened my mouth to say something, thought better of it, turned, and dashed down the steps.

I was in full motion, running toward the sidewalk until Daddy hollered from the other side of the street where he was getting in the car: "Frankie, you look both ways before you cross!"

I stopped, remembering that I had a bad habit of running across without looking, and that it had earned me a couple of near-misses with cars coming down Mee Street's hill. Mama and Daddy had fussed at me about that longer than they usually did about things I wasn't supposed to do. No cars were coming, but I stopped and hung back until Mama and Auntie caught up with me at the edge of the sidewalk. I wanted to check Mama's face again. In the car, I wouldn't be able to see it with her in the front passenger seat and me in the back. They came along side of me, and I took Mama's hand, looking up at her face. Nothing. No sign that she was mad. Why didn't she say something? Was she pretending?

In the car, I chewed on my thumbnail, trying to figure out what the grownups were up to. My heart was beating lickety-split. I felt like an ambushed, Army scout surrounded by Indians, and down to his last bullet. The scout knew he was gonna get shot full of arrows and the buzzards would come and eat up his innards. But he had to wait. Waiting was the worst part. For him and for me. As we drove uptown to the Greyhound station on Gay Street, the waiting made me feel like those ugly buzzards were already eating on me. Daddy and Mama talked about the meeting and Auntie kept quiet like she always did around Daddy. Maybe Auntie didn't snitch on me yet. Maybe Mama wasn't pretending. Maybe she didn't know. Maybe Auntie wasn't gonna tell until we got to the bus station.

I peeked at Auntie sitting beside me in the back seat. She was staring straight ahead. A few minutes passed and she said: "Esther."

When she called Mama's name, I jumped like she'd hit me. *Here it comes,* I said to myself, holding my breath.

"Esther, you ain't got no tomatoes to go wit them greens I cooked. An I knows Mr. Lennon and this here girl dotes on having some sliced tomatoes."

"We'll pick some up on the way home, Sister. Thank you for letting me know."

I let my breath out slowly, feeling like John Wayne must have when a bullet whizzed by his head, just missing him. The next thing I knew Daddy was turning into the bus station. He found a parking space, pulled in, and stopped. My lungs felt like they'd run out of air. I was twisting and pulling at my plaits, waiting for Auntie to open her mouth and let it all out, right here, at the last minute.

Mama helped Auntie out of the back seat, and turned to walk with her to the boarding gate, but Auntie held up her hand. This was it. Auntie was getting ready to tell her. I scooted over to the other side of the car, so I could hear every word she was saying.

"No need for you to come, Esther. I kin make it by m'self."

"But, Sister," Mama said, "I always walk you to the gate."

Auntie shook her head; the little gold earrings danced at her ears. "You go on back. I wanta walk by m'self. Mind me, now. Go on." Then, she turned and hobbled toward the bus, leaving Mama staring, open-mouthed, watching her go her way alone.

I let out a shaky breath. Auntie hadn't told. I didn't understand why, but I did understand that I wasn't gonna get spanked, and I wasn't gonna get punished. Relief came so strong that I had to squeeze my legs together to keep from wetting myself.

As I watched Auntie go, for some reason, I remembered one of the things she'd said in the kitchen. *You got as much spunk as yo mama even though them peoples of hers tried to beat it outta her.* Auntie said that she and somebody took Mama in. Did that mean that Auntie and Mama weren't blood? Weren't really sisters? The idea was so confusing that my brain couldn't wrap itself around it. Feeling like everything was turning topsy-turvy, my mind made a grab for something that hadn't changed. Something that was still true. Mama was my real mama. Auntie had good as said so. Said I had *spunk* like Mama. I wondered again what that word meant, but I couldn't ask just yet because I'd have to tell where I'd heard it, and who said it. So, I'd have to wait until next week when I came home from kindergarten, and pretend I'd heard it there.

"Want to hear the radio, Tugg?" Daddy asked, using his pet name for me. That meant he was feeling good. Probably cause Auntie was gone.

"Yes, Daddy. Please."

He switched on the radio, catching the tail end of a toothpaste commercial. Music swelled in the background as the announcer's voice rang out, "And now, back to our program, *The Adversary* starring Dick Powell, with special guest star, Ida Lupino."

That was the word I had tried to remember earlier this afternoon. I repeated it aloud. "Ad, adver, adversary. Tell me again, Daddy. What does it mean?"

For a second, he said nothing as he stared at Auntie's slow hobble toward the gate. I started to ask him again. Then, he answered me: "It means two people who are opponents on opposite sides of the fence. It's almost the same as being rivals, just like when my basketball team plays Pearl High."

"Oh." I thought for a moment, then asked: "Is it like being enemies?"

Daddy nodded. "In a way, yeah."

I wondered what it was between me and Auntie that made us adversaries. Maybe it was like they said in the cowboy movies—that there was bad blood between us. Whatever that meant. But was there really? After all, she didn't tell on me. And why didn't she? Trying to figure that out was like trying to make the pieces of my puzzle fit right. Only a lot harder. Grownups, to me, were a mystery. And figuring them out would take forever. But I had figured out that if Auntie and Mama weren't blood kin, then that meant me and Auntie weren't blood either. I wondered, for a moment, if Daddy knew. But the wondering flew out of my mind when Daddy sneaked me a bag of M&M's. I tore them open and popped a handful of sweet chocolate in my mouth before Mama could see and say I'd spoil my supper. M&M's were my favorites. Right up there next to Hershey bars.

Plaits

1. Worm Salad

"Ouch! Oww! That hurts!" I moaned as Mama tugged at the comb stuck in my hair. It was early Saturday morning and we were in my room. Mama was sitting on my bed while I was on my little brown chair, wedged between her legs, a squiggling, squirming six-year old. Mama really wasn't hurting me. At least not like Auntie did when she combed my hair; Auntie yanked my head this and thataway when she combed, pulling the little tangly strands so hard that tears sprung into my eyes. I was really hollering because I didn't like what Mama was doing to my hair.

"Stop moving, Frankie," Mama said with just enough something in her voice to make me simmer down to a quiet pout. I couldn't see her, but I knew her vanilla-cream face had tightened up. And I knew not to cross her.

Instead of the usual three plaits, one on top, two in the back, she was braiding my hair into a jillion, itty-bitty, snaky plaits again. Why was she doing it? This many plaits made me look like Buckwheat or Topsy — the kind of Colored kids that White people put in the movies to make fools of. Plaits made me think of those movie pictures of raggedy, little Colored children with hair looking ratty-nasty and standing on end. Little Colored children with porcupine hair and cherry-red lips, slurpin up watermelon and grinnin to beat the band. Who wanted to look like that? Not me. I wanted Shirley Temple's hair. Me and a million other Colored girls.

"Mama, why can't I get Shirley Temple curls?" I whined, feeling sorry for myself.

"You'll get them for the kindergarten play. Soon. I promise." She continued to part, oil, brush, and plait my dark brown hair.

Little Miss Shirley Temple was a movie star and America's sweetheart. She was Goldilocks in the flesh. A creamy-skinned, golden-haired, nursery school wonder that sang and danced her way into the hearts of one and all. At least that's what they said on the radio. She was all sweetness and light, they said. A lily-white lovely. A miniature beauty whose hair was a dream of sun-kissed curls—Shirley Temple curls—that bounced and swayed whenever she tap-danced. Her hair was like the Golden Fleece—a prize, a trophy hard sought after at the beauty shop. Every little blackberry, chocolate, ginger, butterscotch, sweet-cream Colored girl, every one of us wished she would wake up to find that her wiry, corkscrewed locks had turned magically into Shirley's straight, blonde, silky curls. Her hair, they said, was the best: Good hair. Our hair, they said, was the worst: Bad hair. Topsy-hair. We wanted the good. The curls that would bounce in the wind. Flow through your fingers. Feel like silk.

In the picture books that Mama bought me, all the fairies had Shirley-hair. And, in our kindergarten play, I was going to be a Dew Drop Fairy, one with curls that bobbed and bounced every time you moved your head. Maybe, I would even get to wave a wand around and say magic spells, like Cinderella's godmother. But for sure, I would get to wear a satiny costume with some sparkly stuff. Because I had seen Mama sewing it on her Singer machine, pumping the foot pedal to make it go.

Anticipation skipped happily through my head. Mama had promised me Shirley-hair, and everybody knew that with Shirley-hair, you were beautiful. It made you that way. I wished I could wear Shirley-hair everyday instead of these ole plaits Mama was always giving me. They made me ugly! I sighed, deep into self-pity.

Outside my window, I could hear my playmates playing Hide 'n Seek in the spring sunshine. Someone was calling the numbers, "Ten, 'leven, twelve, thirteen, fourteen, fifteen. All hid?" It was Jerry. He couldn't count to a hundred, only to fifteen. Then he had to start all over again.

I frowned, wishing Mama would be finished. I wanted to go outside and play. "Please, Mama, can't you hurry up?"

"You just hold your horses, young lady. Your friends at The Square will have to wait because your hair is breaking off and I have to do more than the usual three plaits. You want to look pretty, don't you?" Humming, Mama reached into the brown bag, rattling around among the clothespins. "Ahh," she said in a satisfied tone, pulling one out, "blue; just the color I wanted." She clamped it on the end of my plait.

I kept quiet. Pretty? How was I gonna be pretty in plaits? Bad enough that she was fixing my hair that way, but then she had to go and anchor them down with plastic, colored clothespins to keep my hair from coming undone. Ugh! Nobody else had to wear those ugly things. Across the room, just to the left of my dressing table, there was a large, standing mirror. I was scared to look, but curiosity won because I wanted to see what she was doing. I watched her pull out a red bow barrette from the bag and fix it at the side of my head near the top. This was something new. Clothespins and now barrettes, too, clinging to all those snaky-looking, little plaits. I sighed again. Shirley's hair never looked like a worm salad.

2. At The Square

Half an hour later, I was walking across the street to my playmates. I couldn't run because of the noise the clothespins made. If I ran, the clothespins clanked. Loudly. Constantly. Doing a fast tap dance on my head. If I speeded up and shifted into sprinter or road runner speed, those suckers turned into lethal weapons; they were like mini versions of Joe Louis, slapping and slugging me upside the head.

At The Square, some of the girls were jumping rope while they chanted. The boys were at the far end playing Dodge Ball. In the sandbox, Evelyne and Shirley were digging and building something. Their hair was in plaits, too. Only their mamas gave them the standard three, like most of the mamas did. Shirley's hair was thicker and longer than mine and Evelyne's was the shortest of us three. They didn't seem to mind the plaits on their heads. Or the barrettes. But then their mamas didn't put a zillion plaits in their hair either.

They glanced up as I squatted down into the sand with them. Neither of them said anything about my hair although Shirley had a funny look on her sugarplum face and Evelyne rolled her sad, brown eyes. That was as close as they would get to saying something about the plaits Mama had given me. I was really glad, too, because I'd peeked at myself after Mama finished. She called herself matching up the clothespins and barrettes with what I was wearing. I looked a mess. What were those words Mama used to describe things that looked a mess? I remembered: hodge and podge. That's what I looked like, a hodge and podge. All red and yellow and blue from head to toe. Like somebody's rainbow-colored porcupine. I knew it might get me teased if anybody really noticed. I hated being teased. It was plain meanness to make fun of somebody.

For a while, nobody took notice. I'd almost forgotten myself how my head looked. We were too busy in the sandbox making cakes and pies, along with sandcastles and tunnels. Then James, who was visiting his cousin, Shirley, came running over. He spied me and screeched to a stop like Jackie Robinson sliding to home base. He screwed up his eyes and stared at me like I was a two-headed wonder. I tried to wish myself invisible, even got up to try to make for the far corner of The Square. I just wanted to avoid what was coming. But it was no use. He zeroed in.

"Hey, hey! Look at Buckwheat over here," he hollered, pointing my way. My heart stopped beating. To us, calling somebody Buckwheat was the worst kind of name-calling. It was the same as calling you Black Baboon, Little Black Sambo, or Monkey Girl. Those names low-rated you really bad. At this, Evelyne and Shirley looked at me and then at each other, their faces breaking up into helpless giggles. The rest of the kids turned around, did a double take, and then fell to the ground, laughing so hard that tears ran down their cheeks.

Tears ran down my cheeks, too. Only I wasn't laughing. I was burning with shame. I wanted to jump down James' throat and beat his head into mashed potatoes. But Mama didn't allow fighting; if I did, she'd whip me 'til I couldn't sit. So I did the only thing that I knew to protect myself. I ran away. To safety. Back to my house. Mama was cooking in the kitchen so she didn't know I was crying when I ran in, and Daddy had gone to the store. Alone in my room, I quietly bawled my eyes out.

3. Cooked Goose

That night after my parents tucked me into bed, I feigned sweet dreams until I figured they had slipped off to sleep city. At the sound of Daddy snoring, I crept to the entrance to their bedroom, hesitating there for a few seconds just to make sure they were asleep. All I needed to do was keep quiet as a church mouse and go in without waking them up. I knew where to find what I needed. I had checked the dresser drawer in their bedroom earlier when I'd made up my mind to do it. I wasn't going to let what happened with James ever happen again if I could help it. I knew what I had to do.

With my parents dreaming a few feet away, I tiptoed to the dressing table. It was very dark and I could barely make out the outlines of the furniture. I could just see where I was going, stepping carefully because if I stumbled and woke them, my goose would be cooked. They'd never believe whatever story I came up with to explain why I was in their room. At the dresser, ever so slowly, I pulled the drawer out, and, quietly, felt around for the scissors among the lipsticks, cream jars, and other stuff. My fingertips touched the handles and I grabbed. Relieved to have found them, I let out a soft, long breath. Then I stopped to listen to Mama and Daddy. They were still asleep; their breathing said so. In a frenzy to be done with it now, I sat down on the floor, seizing the offending plaits, and went to work on right side of my head. Plaits dropped into the lap of my nightgown like blessings from heaven. I smiled to myself in the dark. It was going just like I planned. Soon as I finished with the right side, I started on the left, and that's when Daddy let out a big, loud snort. It scared me so bad I almost wet myself. I stopped what I was doing and listened. Did he wake himself up? A few breathless moments, then he went back to snoring. By now, though, I had chickened. I took a few more snips before gathering the plaits up in my nightgown to sneak out. Back in my room, sleep pushed at my eyelids. I dumped the hair in my wastebasket and climbed into bed without looking in the mirror.

The next morning when Daddy came in to wake me, he blinked, and then gaped as I lifted my head from the pillow. "Estelle," he bellowed, "you better come in here." He whistled softly and shook his head.

I stumbled out of bed as Mama came in. Daddy had melted back into another part of the house. He was protecting his flanks from the fallout that he figured was sure to come.

Her dark eyes widened as she came toward me. "I don't know what got into you, young lady, but you've really done it now," she said, standing in front of me.

I stood my ground. "No more iddy, biddy plaits with clothes pins for me," I said by way of some kind of defiant explanation.

Mama looked at me hard. Her face threatening to turn into thunderclouds. *Here it comes.* I just knew she was gonna wear me out with a switch.

She reached out and fingered what was left of my hair. "You look like a half-plucked chicken. Do you realize you're going to have to live with how you look until your hair grows back?"

I hadn't looked in the mirror yet. But now, I turned to face what I'd done. For a second, I didn't recognize the little butterscotch-faced girl I saw staring back with tattered hair. Blindly and brutally, I'd hacked, chopped, and pared away all of the hair on the right side. What was left—an inch of hair here, two inches there—stuck out at odd angles. As for the left, after Daddy's snort had scared me, I'd rushed to finish and had only taken a couple of swipes at it. So most of the plaits were still there except for a couple near my ear that I'd hacked off halfway.

I turned from the mirror, swallowing hard. I had goofed, but I was gonna stand my ground. Take my punishment without a peep.

"I don't think you need a whipping," Mama said.

No whipping? A relieved grin spread across my face.

Mama saw the little grin and shook her head. "I guess you haven't realized it, yet, Frankie. But you've cooked your own goose. You forgot," Mama said, "while you were getting rid of your iddy, biddy plaits that your kindergarten play is in three weeks."

Three weeks? My mind sputtered over the words.

"I don't think," Mama went on, "that Mrs. Johnson is going to be able to make any Shirley Temple curls out of what's left of your butchered hair. It looks a mess!" Then she walked out of my room, leaving me to think about her last remark.

No Shirley Temple curls? My heart sunk like a stone in water.

Slowly, I turned to look at myself in the mirror again. The stubs of my wiry hair were sticking out all over the place. My lower lip trembled as I looked at my reflection. As the crocodile tears that had welled up in my eyes began rolling, ever so slowly, down my cheeks, I thought to myself with bitter regret: *Whoever heard of a Dew Drop Fairy with Topsy-hair!*

Woman Dreams:
Going Against the Grain

I fell hopelessly in love with the movies before I reached the age of six. Armed with popcorn, hot ham sandwiches, Hershey bars, and grape soda, I settled down every Saturday afternoon at the Gem Theater where I gorged myself on a steady diet of Bugs Bunny cartoons, Our Gang, The Three Stooges, Bela Lugosi vampire thrillers, or Jimmy Cagney gangster tales. When I was small, my favorites were shoot-'em-ups, starring tall, tough John Wayne, and the Republic Pictures serials, featuring action-adventure heroes like Spy Smasher and Rocket Man. I was endlessly fascinated that this week the hero perished at the end of the reel only to be resurrected next time through some miraculous escape. As I got older, my favorites became MGM musicals with dancers like sexy, red-haired Rita Hayworth, or dark-haired, curvaceous Cyd Charisse who sent me home dreaming about becoming a dancer. And other things.

What flashed across the screen in coded symbols and metaphors gave me subtle instructions. In matters of femininity and masculinity. In matters of skin color and beauty. In matters of sex and desire. And, in that which was forbidden. There, in the darkness, Hollywood's magic lantern constructed a palace of dreams where the White screen goddesses of the day reigned supreme. The camera's golden eye made them irresistible: It caressed and lovingly magnified every curve of the chin, breast, and hip. And so,

51

I began to learn what was desirable. And, gradually, what I desired. Since the silver screen never placed Black women in the firmament of stars, I came to favor what it showed me. I came to favor, not the sweet, simple-minded blondes, but the dark-haired femme fatales—the bad girls who were gutsy and headstrong. Like Susan Hayward, clever and untamable. Hedy Lamarr, mysterious and tantalizing. Ava Gardner, dangerous and unpredictable, or Jane Russell, wanton and voluptuous. Every one of them the sirens of men's dreams. And mine.

When I was growing up, Hollywood taught me that desire was one thing, but its fulfillment was a secretive matter—something hidden behind the closed doors of the bawdy house, or discreetly placed behind a boudoir curtain, places where the camera never went. As a kid, I never thought twice about the closed doors, but as time went on, I wondered: What was this thing called sexual attraction? What went on behind those closed doors? What was so mysterious, so forbidden about sex? Why was it padlocked and rendered invisible? Hollywood would not show me the answers. Except in symbol and sign. The answers were taboo. Which, of course, gave them the kind of mystical power that only things banished as taboo can acquire. Sex was a coded enigma.

The advent of my menstrual period, at age eleven, in the sixth grade, threatened, suddenly, to render the matter visible. Visible, at least, in my house. For a moment, I thought I'd get a clue about this mysterious and forbidden thing. I wanted to be in the know since bleeding, sex, and boys were the hot topics on the playground at lunchtime. But that was not to be. In typical parental fashion, Mama announced that I needed to know about sex now that I had gotten my period. To explain it all, she handed me a book that pictured strange looking internal organs which reportedly were somewhere in the vicinity of my "private parts." Said book dutifully told me that I could expect blood to flow monthly because of some egg dropping from somewhere—a process I could only liken to jelly beans dropping out of the Gem Theater's candy machine after I'd put my penny in. Having put the book in my hands, she warned me to be a lady and always, "Keep your dress down and your legs closed." Thus, my home lesson in Sex 101 was completed, leaving me still in the dark.

In the dark. Where Hollywood whetted and teased my appetite about sex. In the dark. About why I was dreaming of stunning Rita Hayworth and Ava Gardner, instead of bad-ass John Wayne or brawny Burt Lancaster. At some point, I don't remember when, I began to wonder if other girls dreamed like I did, not of men, but of women. I didn't know and I wasn't going to ask. Though I wanted to. I wanted to ask one of my friends if, at night, before falling off to sleep, she made up romantic little scripts in her head like I did. My nighttime scenarios cast as my leading lady whichever Hollywood knockout had, lately, taken my fancy. I, of course, would imagine myself all aglitter in magnificent gowns, shoes, furs, and jewels, cozily ensconced in a Manhattan penthouse apartment, courtesy of money's mammy. My script would lay out the usual wooing with a bit of music and some lovely dancing, like those Ginger Rodgers and Fred Astaire movies that I dearly loved; after I won my lady love's heart, the scenario inevitably ended with us pledging our love. The pledge was always sealed with my bestowing passionate, fiery kisses upon my pillow-lover. It was my secret movie production. A forbidden drama. Played out in the shadows of dark.

Later, I would decode the symbols on the silver screen, would begin to learn certain lessons. Hollywood would teach me about what was forbidden. About what was taboo in the dark, as well as the light. About what happens when you go against the grain.

On my twelfth birthday, I celebrated by taking five of my girlfriends to the movies at the Bijou, located downtown, the White part of Knoxville. I really hated the Bijou because us Black folks had to climb their steep, narrow steps to sit in the balcony, while Whites sat, in Jim Crow privilege, on the ground floor. Unlike the Gem, the Bijou got first and second run movies, and it was showing *Carmen Jones*, a musical with an all Black cast. I'd never seen a movie with an all Black cast; plus, the movie poster of star, Dorothy Dandridge, had set me on fire. She was bad. She was beautiful. And she was Black. I just had to see the movie, so we were going.

I was almost breathless with excitement as Daddy drove to pick up the other five girls and headed for the Bijou. I don't remember exactly which of my friends I invited; it was probably Janice, Beatrice, Charlene, Judy, and Rosalyn. After we marched into the postage stamp-sized lobby, Daddy bought us bags of popcorn and cold drinks. I was nearly dancing in anticipation. As he was paying, one of my friends checked me out, saw that I was hopping from one foot to the other, and asked if I had to use the bathroom. I shook my head and promptly shut down my racing motor. Then, we climbed those mountainous steps to the crow's nest, which was what somebody nicknamed the balcony. I led the way inside. There were, I think, a few couples hugged up and groping each other in the rear rows, but I ignored them, and headed for the front row, thanking my lucky stars that it was empty that day. I wanted to be front and center when Dorothy Dandridge came on screen with no knuckleheads blocking my view.

Years later, when Hollywood made a movie of Dandridge's life, Halle Berry played Dorothy Dandridge. I understand why Berry was cast. Halle Berry is very pretty, but she can't hold a candle, in my opinion, to Dandridge.

Dandridge was knock-down-drag-out beautiful. It's the eyes, I think, that make the difference between them. Berry's eyes are lamb's innocence. Dandridge's eyes were those of a woman who knew all about temptation and seduction. Her eyes invited you to drown in them, if you dared.

It was those eyes that drew you in her first scene as Carmen. Dressed in high heels, a tight red skirt with a split up the side, a black peasant blouse, huge, silver hoop earrings, you could believe she was a gypsy woman—the Queen of Gypsies. Every move—the casual shrug of shoulder, the toss of hair, the teasing smile, and those flashing eyes—every move told you that she was going to take Joe, the soldier, down in a New York minute. I knew Joe (played by Harry Belafonte) was a fool when he thought that being engaged would protect him from Carmen. Because she had set her cap to get him, and I knew she would. It amused her that he tried to resist her. He'd fall, she knew, and his fiancée, Cindy Lou, be damned. As the movie unfolded, I was just as much bewitched with her as poor Joe came to be. Dandridge playing Carmen was all those things that my mother had dared not speak of. Fire. And Desire with a capital D. By the time I came up for air, somebody had eaten all my popcorn and the ice in my Pepsi had melted. I didn't care. I was smitten.

I particularly remember the scene where Joe leaves the base and comes to Carmen's shack. Though he tries not to show it, Joe wants her badly—enough to play out on his fiancé, enough to grovel to Carmen. As I watched them dance around each other, I began to understand something of the game they were playing with each other. He is almost limp with desire, and she knows it. She wants him, too, yet she is trapped in the game of wanting that requires her to taunt and tease him before she gives in.

Before she will allow them both to fulfill their desire for each other. Here was a lesson: Sex required you to tease, required you to taunt, required you to play out a ritual before you went behind the closed doors to break the taboo. To act on desire.

Once they do act, they are doomed. She can't be happy with Joe because she wants to live the lush life that only lots of money can buy, and he has no money. I was sad about that part because I wanted them to be happy forever after. As I watched the movie, I wondered: Were they doomed because they'd done something forbidden when they gave in to desire? Were they doomed because they went against the grain? Because Joe had jilted Cindy Lou, and now they had to pay for being bad? Probably so, I thought. Being twelve, after all, is to live in the land of naiveté and I had no concept of Joe and Carmen being caught in the briar patch of being poor and Black. No concept that poverty made you hungry for things that can never fill you up.

Soon, Carmen finds someone with money—a boxer, and she leaves Joe for him. At the end of the movie, Joe kills her for that. Chokes the life out of her. That scene put me in shock. There she is, on her way to her ringside seat, dressed in a fabulous, strapless white gown and a white ermine; there she is looking, for all the world, a million times better than Rita or Jane who never got killed at the end of a movie. I couldn't believe he was doing it— choking her to death. I was outdone and I cried. Because I thought she was too beautiful to die, and because he cries himself after he does the deed. All I knew was I wanted them to live happily ever after, no matter what. I wanted them to win. But the house won instead and I took note of that.

Although I could not have verbalized these things then, I had, that day, absorbed and decoded subtle messages on the screen. Messages about the pursuit of love and sex and desire. Messages about breaking taboos, and punishments exacted for the breaking. Messages about Black women. About their love lives. And their fate.

In the car, on the way to Carter-Roberts, the drugstore and soda shop where Daddy was taking us for ice cream sodas, Rosalyn and Janice laughed at me for crying at the end of the movie, and that started everyone chattering. Belafonte, they said, was "fine-as-wine" and Dandridge, "just plain gorgeous." Silently, I added a dozen more superlatives about her. As far as I was concerned, she'd blown the other Hollywood irresistibles out of the water, and gone straight to the top of the screen goddess pantheon. I had fallen for her—hook, line, and sinker.

I would remember certain things about that movie in years to come. Remember the sexual game that required Carmen to put aside desire, and, instead, tease and torment the man who wanted her. Remember that both became prisoners of their wanting. I remembered because, later on, I became a prisoner, too, required to hide, required to put aside my own desires, unable to pursue and resolve them. As time passed, somehow, in my mind, that movie became a signal event for me, defining things taboo. Defining limits and boundaries that you cross at your peril.

Although the grungy, old Gem Theater is gone now, somewhere, in a universe unbound by linear time, it's Saturday and I'm at the Gem, eating popcorn and Hershey bars, rooting for Rocket Man, and laughing at The Three Stooges. I am there in the dark, waiting anxiously. Waiting for the camera to show me the next woman that will inhabit my dreams.

The Code

I grew up with a lot of "aunts." They were my parents' friends, my mother's in particular. I suppose that my mother came up with the title "aunt" as a way for me to show respect and affection in a "proper" way to her friends, for the custom of the Black community of the 1950's never allowed children to address adults by their first names.

That would have broken The Code. The Code, by the way, was an interlocking system of customs, rules, and values officially adopted as *The Way We Do It Here* by Knoxville's Black folk. To subscribe to The Code brought you inside the fold—inside the community. Nobody wanted to be an outsider, excommunicated, if you will, from the fold. So you subscribed. And although sometimes it could be suffocating or painful, I think that was a good thing in many ways.

My no-relation aunts flowered the landscape of my childhood; they linger in my mind like the sweet, summer smell of honeysuckle. Aunt Teri, who lived in Cincinnati, raising a girl, four boys, and a husband, was my summertime, visiting aunt—the one with the throaty laugh who wore magnificent high heels and seamed, embroidered stockings. I adored her. To me she was just as much a Black goddess as Hollywood's Lena Horne or Dorothy Dandridge. When my mother took me shopping for my first pair of high-heeled shoes, I searched for and bought that special pair that I thought Aunt Teri would buy. Every time I wore them, I imagined myself as elegant and sexy as she.

And then, there was redheaded Aunt Lil, the elementary school music teacher who struggled heroically to teach me the finer points of piano playing. Music lessons, my mother believed, were absolutely necessary to my becoming a "lady." I didn't like memorizing Bach and Brahms, but I did like hanging out with my confidante, Aunt Lil. She indulged my obsession with her rhinestone and crystal jewelry, listened to my secrets while brewing me pots of exotic-tasting sassafras tea, and introduced me to the driving rhythms of Count Basie's "One O'clock Jump."

My favorite "real" aunt was Claire, who was married to my father's brother, Madison. Aunt Claire was a ritual-keeper. As I moved through each stage toward adulthood, she marked the passage with a celebration and remembrance of some sort. Back in those days, unlike today, aunts and mothers and grandmothers did not allow the advertising world to seduce young girls into buying items of womanhood at a tender, under-ripe age. It was Aunt Claire who gave me my first real grown-up perfume, Chanel Number 5, when I was sixteen. "Only women wear this scent," she told me as she presented it. Because it came from Aunt Claire (and in a way from my mother since I knew she'd given her consent that I could receive it), I have never forgotten how loved I felt at that moment. I was growing up and that fact was being recognized with this gift of initiation and welcome from the women.

They were the Glenda-the-Good aunts. But this story isn't about them. This story is about the diva. The aunt I didn't like: Helen. I didn't like her, among other reasons, because she took every opportunity to badmouth my mother and, most of the time, she did it in front of other people. Aunt Helen's withering comments about Mama were relentless. She just never stopped. Curiously enough, my mother never talked about the silent war Aunt Helen seemed to always be waging against her, nor did anyone else in the family. Black people in Knoxville sure knew how to keep a secret (and there were enough to keep a soap opera writer in juicy scripts for years), so whoever might have known the complete history of the Helen versus Estelle conflict kept mum.

My mother would certainly have disapproved of what I'm saying here—washing the family's dirty linen in public as it were. But I'm not my mother. I'm probably more like my father when it comes to linen, so I'll hang out some more dirt. A very tender bone of contention between Mama and Aunt Helen was quite likely Daddy's drinking and partying. Which Aunt Helen encouraged at every opportunity. And there were many such opportunities because she lived right next door where she and her motley crew were almost always partying.

Although in her youth Aunt Helen had been trained as a registered nurse, she later retired to become a full-time wife to my father's oldest brother, Uncle Frank, who was one of a handful of Black doctors in segregated Knoxville. That fact, I think, went to her head. In the fashion of notorious and self-indulgent divas everywhere, she surrounded herself with a crew of what would be known today as groupies. Almost every day, they gathered in her kitchen which was huge enough to comfortably accommodate a dozen people. There, the groupies scraped, bowed, and worshipped Aunt Helen, not from afar, but quite near.

Despite the fact that Aunt Helen was fat and short, she was ever the formidable foe, perpetually armed with the haughty expression; I see her now—the grand dame moving about her kitchen putting on Nat King Cole's record, "Nature Boy," while she whipped up Uncle Frank's dinner. Today, perhaps a Black Forest cake, homemade vanilla ice cream, a ragout of beef with a wicked, rum-laced sweet potato casserole and fresh (Never canned!) green beans on the side. Her meals were a triumph. And she went about making each one as if she were a contender going for the gold. When it came to cooking, she took no prisoners; anyone who might, however remotely, be a threat to her domain, she dispatched with the unerring instincts of a heat-seeking missile. I should know for I remember our duel in the afternoon. That skirmish burned in my gut for years.

My mother had insisted that I bake a cake for Uncle Frank's birthday. After all, I was his namesake and, at twelve years old, I was just learning to cook. It would be a special gesture, she told me, if I put in the effort to make him a birthday cake on my own. I tried to stonewall my way around Mama's idea. Put simply, I really dreaded baking this cake. This was Aunt Helen's territory and I knew she was fiercely jealous of it. But as anyone who knew my mother can tell you, once Estelle Lennon made up her mind, she was like a hound put to scent. Nothing could shake her single-minded resolve. So there I was— caught between the hound on scent and the heat-seeking missile.

I can still see Aunt Helen peering at me through her gold-rimmed glasses as I carefully stepped into her kitchen that afternoon, holding the cake out in front of me. The kitchen crew, sans Daddy, were there; some listening to jazz while they brown-nosed Aunt Helen; others chopping celery, basting meat, shucking corn, readying the ingredients for The Chef de Cuisine to prepare the masterpiece, birthday dinner. On one of the kitchen counters, I spied a triple-layered, Lady Baltimore Snow

Cake—Aunt Helen's famous specialty. My knees quaked as I presented my double-layered, chocolate cake.

"This is for Uncle Frank's birthday," I told Aunt Helen.

Everyone in the room stopped. Even the record player went silent. All eyes riveted on me. I gulped.

"Put it there," Aunt Helen said, pointing to the empty space next to the Lady Baltimore. I put the cake down. Then I looked at it. Sitting beside Lady Baltimore, mine seemed a bit lopsided; even worse, the swirling peaks of the chocolate frosting were sliding down the sides. Obviously, I hadn't mastered frosting yet.

I remember a ghost of a smile—probably more like a smirk—played round Aunt Helen's lips as she tilted her head slightly to the side, regarding my cake with pity.

"Tell me the recipe for your cake," she purred, setting her trap with care.

Without missing a beat, I walked right into it. "It's Pillsbury."

There was an audible gasp from the motley crew. My cake wasn't made from "scratch" but came out of a box. I had committed a sin of the first order in Aunt Helen's world of haute cuisine.

She had me now and she pounced. "You made your uncle a box cake?" She glanced at the cake once more, turning up her nose at it. "Well," she turned away from me to address her motley crew, "what can you expect? Her mother can't cook herself, so how's the child to learn?" She gave my cake a look of disdain and burst out laughing. Following suit, the motley crew tittered.

My face froze with shame and anger. I could see that Aunt Helen was pleased with herself; the threat to her domain had been summarily dealt with. I had been properly shot down, put in my place, vanquished on the battlefield. She had won the day.

And she knew it. I was just a kid bound by The Code—which meant that I couldn't fight back. If I gave her some smart lip, I'd be breaking the rules. And that would reflect poorly in everyone's eyes on how my mother was bringing me up. Worse still, to break The Code would make me the bad guy in the eyes of the community. At that moment, I could only keep silent and get the hell out of her kitchen before I burst into tears. The shame burned inside me for a long time.

Looking back, I know for sure that, in that instance, I was caught between a rock and a hard place. Had I broken The Code, I would have gotten a hellavu whipping from my mother and a no television-no movies punishment as well. My mother was one strong believer in The Code. As for Aunt Helen, you could say that she had the good life, but it didn't seem to make her happy. She was a lifelong backbiter. Uncle Frank finally divorced her—*and wasn't that a scandal!*—because back then divorce went against The Code. When I remember Aunt Helen, the kindest comment I can make is that she would never have won the Miss Congeniality award from anybody. Years later, when I was on summer break from graduate school, my father dragged me to a visit with her. Alone and without her motley crew, she was still a vindictive woman—protected, to the bitter end, by The Code.

The Party

"Please, Lord," I whispered under my breath, "don't let that boy ask me to dance." Panic wormed its way through my chest as I sat huddled in the corner, trying to melt into the living room wall of Pepper's house. A record by James Brown and the Famous Flames was playing. Pepper and Jeffrey were wrapped so tightly in each other's arms slow dancing that they looked glued together. In the dim light, the other three couples on the dance floor were grinding to James Brown's wailing ballad: Boy leg pushed between girl leg; boy hips pressed into girl hips. Dancing like that could lead to things getting outta hand. And that thought made me even more nervous because I was supposed to be paired off with the boy slumped on the couch across the room.

I sneaked a look at him. Bobby was his name. His eyes were almost hidden under the black, baseball cap pulled down on his head. There was a dimple in his chin and he had a full-lips that stayed set in a little arrogant smile. Before he could catch me looking at him, I dropped my eyes, smoothed an imaginary wrinkle out of my red pleated skirt, and tucked my legs under my chair. I tried to think of an excuse if he did ask me. I could say: *Nope, can't; my boyfriend don't want me dancin with other boys.* That one wouldn't work. Even though I was in the eighth grade, it was common knowledge at school that I didn't have a boyfriend. My mind worried at it: Maybe I could say I didn't know how or that dancing's against my religion. But those excuses were out too. Pepper and the other girls knew better. Maybe I could say I'm sick or— *Damn! How did I get in this?*

My straight-up-tell-it-like-it-is voice chimed in: *Girl, you know how. Quit actin stupid!*

Yeah, I knew. I was Pepper's Goodie-Two-Shoes cover. Her mama had left for work tonight thinking we were practicing our dance number so we could be in the Vine Jr. Talent Night next week. Soon as she left, here comes Patty, Janice, and Rita. We were all in the same homeroom, and I knew they were Pepper's main runnin buddies. I smelled trouble right then. Then seems like two seconds after they showed up, here come their high school boyfriends with one extra boy for me, so everybody could get paired off and do Lord-have-mercy-knows-what. Which was fine for them, but I didn't know this Bobby from Adam. Inviting Bobby had to be Pepper's big idea. I suddenly felt hot with anger. *How she think I'ma be with somebody I don't know? What she think she doin, hookin me up like that?* I listened for a comeback from the voice. Not a peep.

It didn't have to bother this time. Truth be told, since sixth grade, Pepper had been makin it her business to hook me up with a boyfriend. First one she'd tried to set me up with was pretty-eyed Jeremy. Had him walking me home from Eastport School every day. Actually, I'd walk so fast that he had to trail behind me. It went on for three weeks til I couldn't stand it no more and told him my Mama wouldn't like him walkin me home if she found out. It was a lie but it scared him off for good.

Then last year, Pepper had said: "You and Anthony would be a cute couple."

Cute couple, my butt! Nobody asked me what I thought! But Pepper had done made her mind up to put Anthony on me. And he was a whole lot harder to put off than Jeremy. Make matters worse, seem like everybody in seventh grade wanted him and me to be together, and they was plottin and plannin how to pull it off. So, I had to use extreme actions to get him off me. I turned stone cold on him. Wouldn't talk to him or even look his way. Never mind the intense, puppy dog looks he'd give me all day at school. Wore me out so much that I almost gave up and gave in. Then, one afternoon after school, I saw him and Jeanie at her locker, and he was grinnin at her all lovesick like while he tucked her books under his arm; then as they walked out the door, she grabbed his hand and squeezed it. That's when I knew I was saved. No Anthony for me. *Thank you, Lord!*

Remembering all that made me cut my eyes at Pepper even though she didn't see me give her that nasty look. The music was over and she wasn't studyin nobody but Jeffrey right then. She had a silly grin stretched from ear to ear cause she'd finally got his attention after tryin to rope him in since last year. They say opposites attract and to look at them together you'd sure think so. She was high yella, like me, with thick, auburn hair; he had skin as dark and smooth as hot chocolate and a killer smile.

"Frankie," Pepper's voice jolted me out of my thoughts. "how come you and Bobby didn't dance?" Her auburn brows always knitted together in a funny way, like they did now, when she was puzzled.

Though I tried to keep from blushing, I could feel the heat in my face, and before I could stammer out an answer, Bobby said: "I ain't asked her to dance yet." His voice sounded stony and hard.

Pepper opened her mouth to follow up on that one, but Jeffrey pulled her to him and kissed her long and hard right in front of us. The boys started to whistle, catcall, and stomp their feet. The girls just giggled. While they were distracted, I made a quick getaway to the kitchen, praying nobody would ask me where I was going. Nobody did.

When I stepped foot in the kitchen, it felt like I had made it home free. Pepper's Mama always kept a kitchen that was so clean it looked like nobody lived there. Mrs. Moore could burn good and every night, she left dinner on the stove for Pepper and her brother. I went to the stove and peeped in the pots: Roast beef, potatoes, onions, and carrots in one; in the other, green beans. It was dinnertime and, ordinarily, my stomach would be talking to me. But hunger wasn't showin up tonight. It was butterflies instead, making themselves right at home in the pit of my stomach.

What am I gonna do when they all start pairin off to do some serious stuff? I thought, worried, and sat down at the table.

The voice answered me: *You could leave.*

Yeah, I could. And I knew I should. My mama would have a fit if she knew what was going on over here. Kill me deader than a doornail. I could see her now, a dangerously black look on her vanilla-crème face, tight little lines around her thin lips; her eyes looking like a tornado was gonna jump out, pick you up and shake you silly.

Didn't matter that I didn't know ahead of time what Pepper had cooked up. I'd still be wrong in her eyes because she'd ask me: "Why didn't you leave, Frankie? Why didn't you just come home? Why did you stay in a house with no chaperone, four other girls and five boys?"

And I wouldn't have an answer for her. Didn't have one for myself either. Why was I stayin?

The voice jumped in and added: *Especially since you don't wanna be here anyway.*

Truth was, I didn't have the nerve to walk out. If I left, it'd be like saying I don't care if you never invite me to nothin else. And I did care cause I wanted to be included. I needed to be. Because something weird was goin on with me. For a long time now. And it was different than what was happening with the other girls. They thought about boys all the time. I didn't. They thought about getting a boyfriend all the time. And I wondered where did it say I had to have a boyfriend?

Sometimes, in the quiet, I could feel something like a presence, hunkering down inside me, just waiting. That's when I'd try to push it back deep down. Just act like it wasn't there. Because I didn't want to know it or name it. So even though I was scared Pepper's mama might come back and catch us, and then Mama would find out and I'd be a dead duck—that wasn't the worse thing. If I left, somebody might guess about what was inside me and call its name. So I wasn't gonna leave this party cause I had to stay. I had to pretend, so nobody would guess.

Right then, as if somebody had cued him, Bobby walked into the kitchen.

"Pepper said to find out where you went." He'd taken off his cap and I could see his eyes—light brown with a cool, direct gaze that could make you feel naked.

Seeing him made me feel panicky again. Why didn't Pepper mind her own business? I wasn't ready to talk to anybody yet, let alone him. Conflicting feelings churned inside me. What to do? I fidgeted with my hair as Bobby sat down facing me at the opposite end of the table.

If I you're gonna to stay, the voice said, *you've gotta pretend.* But I didn't want to pretend. I hated doing that!

"Whatcha doin in here, hiding?" I could tell by his voice that he was teasin me, but there was something else under his tone too, like he really wasn't teasin at all.

"I wanted some water," I lied. He glanced at the empty table. "But I changed my mind," I said.

The voice ridiculed me: *What a lame excuse, girl.*

68

He waited a few beats, then said: "You know, you're a cute girl."

Confusion blanketed my mind. "Thanks," I mumbled, blushing. What was he up to? I was flattered, but I didn't believe him. The mirror told me every day that I was an ordinary-looking Colored girl, just this side of chubby with high cheekbones, a broad nose and full lips. What was cute about that?

He put his arms on the table and leaned toward me. "Yeah, you cute, but you ain't too friendly. Why you act stuck up?"

That hurt my feelings and I wasn't bold enough to give him a smart-mouthed comeback, so I just looked at him. He was silent, staring at me, waiting. The ball was in my court and I was supposed to do something with it.

"I ain't stuck up." My voice shook a little. "I just don't know you, that's all." It sounded lame.

Yeah, said the voice, *everything comin outta your mouth is soundin lame.*

"Well, I can fix that." His lips turned up in a smile, but his eyes didn't match. They still looked like marbles.

A picture popped into my head: Him backing me into the sink, grindin his hips into my hips, pressing his mouth on mine and givin me a soulful kiss. I knew about soulful kisses. That's when a boy stuck his tongue down your throat. The thought gave me the shivers. *Uh, uhn. No way!*

I pushed my chair back hard, and jumped up, shouting: "What's that mean?"

Bobby threw his hands up. "Whoa! Back up! I didn't mean nothin bad," he protested, looking up at me.

I glared at him and took a couple of steps back. I had to do something to mark time. So I walked over to the sink, got a glass, and filled it with water.

It seemed like fifteen or twenty minutes had passed, but it was really only a few seconds until Bobby said, "You awful touchy, girl, you know that?" His voice had a sharpness to it. "When Pepper told me about the party, she said she wanted me to meet somebody cool." He was sayin his words like they was hot off the griddle. "Said you wuz okay, mellowed out," he paused. Then: "You ain't though."

In the living room, somebody played another James Brown record. His voice begged: *Baby, please, please, please, please.* The Flames backed him in smooth, slow drag time. *Baby, please don't go.*

I hated that song. It was Number One on the R&B charts and they played it over and over again at sock hops and parties. Boys asked you to slow dance, held you in a death grip so you couldn't breathe, laid their head against yours, and sweated their way through the song. By the end, you had a stiff neck and a sweated-back, ruined hairstyle. I just hated slow drag songs. As I put my empty glass in the sink, tension made me clench my teeth and I let out a breath to try and ease it.

"You real up tight, Frankie. Whatsa matter, you fraid your boyfriend gonna find out about this?" Before I could say anything, he went on, "Oh, yeah, that's right. Pepper said you ain't got a boyfriend," he paused. It seemed like forever before he went on: "How come you ain't?"

"Ain't what?" I snapped, turning around, praying for an answer to the question I always dreaded.

"Got a boyfriend?" He looked at me speculatively, his eyes sliding down from my face to my chest. His look embarrassed me. I felt like covering my breasts with my arms, but I didn't. His eyes traveled down to my waist, lingered at my hips, and glanced briefly at my legs.

"I dunno," I said. The voice struggled to say something, but I slapped it down. I couldn't meet his gaze, so I stared at the pots on the stove, feeling beads of sweat forming on my belly and under my arms.

"I dunno," he mimicked in a feminine voice. I looked at him. There was a grin on his face, but it wasn't friendly looking. His eyes—they were intense, sharp, like Mama's when she was tryin to see if I was lyin to her. "Most girls be knowin why they ain't got a man. But you don't." He was challenging me to come up with an answer that made sense. I didn't have one.

Then cool as a cucumber, he says to me: "You act like you funny, or something."

Fear slammed into me and my legs went weak. I felt like I wanted to fall down, only those light brown eyes of his had pierced me and was holdin me up. I groped around for something to say, some kinda answer. The voice was still struggling to make me hear it. But I didn't want to. I didn't have time cause I had to think how to say it wasn't true.

"No," I barked at him. "I ain't funny! What kinda thing is that to say to me?" Tears popped into my eyes.

"Reason Pepper told me to come is she say you don't never be round no boys," he went on, his voice rollin over me like a Mac truck.

I wanted to scream for him to stop. I wanted my ears to stop hearing him talk. I wanted to run into the living room and slap Pepper sideways for bringin him here. It was like I was in some horror movie where the monster is comin toward you and you can't move. You can't make a sound. You just stand there and watch it come at you.

Bobby stood up. "Maybe you don't know it, Frankie, but you be actin like you don't like no boys." He started for the kitchen door, was almost there, then paused and looked back at me, his lips curling in a sneer. "I think you one of them—them bulldaggers!" He spat the name out like it had soured his mouth and walked out.

Right then, I felt more scared than I'd ever been in my life cause I didn't know what he'd say to Pepper and them when he got to the living room. I bowed my head in shame, in fear, in confusion as tears rolled down my face and splattered on my sweater. The monster presence was out. He'd named it and I just knew he'd tell. How was I gonna face them? How? My mind went into overdrive. Maybe I could bluff. Play it off. Yeah. Maybe. Cause after all, he couldn't prove what he said. He couldn't. Nobody could. Nobody.

The voice finally got through. It laid the cards on the table: *You know and I know what he said is true. You ain't had no boyfriend cause you didn't want none. Never did and never will.*

I shut it down. Shoved it back deep in a tunnel. Put it down there with the presence. Yeah, that's what I'd do. Bury em both so deep they couldn't never bother me again. In the living room, I heard Pepper and the others laughing. Had he told yet? Maybe not. But I had to find out for sure. I got a napkin, wiped my eyes, and blew my nose. I had to go in there and see. The voice tried to climb back up, but I gave it one last good shove. Pushed it down so deep this time that I knew I wouldn't be able to hear it. And long as I couldn't hear it, I could play this thing off. Walking out of the kitchen, I took a deep breath and braced myself up. I could do it. I just had to remember that nobody could prove what he said was true.

Nobody.

Tales of Jim Crow

When I was coming up, your Mama and Daddy told you trickster stories, like those of B'rer Rabbit or Ananzi, the spider, stories that, for your own good, taught you the tricks of how to survive living with White folks. Since Jim Crow practices were the everyday norm in Knoxville, Tennessee, and elsewhere in the South, back then, you learned from your elders how to let your face and hands and head and shoulders speak in the passive language that White people wanted to hear. You learned that you better wear a mask, put on a blank face that never revealed your feelings. You listened to grown folks whispering about the stories of Colored folk who had to run for their lives in the middle of the night because White men took a notion to put on their white hoods and go coon hunting; you heard about smart-mouthed Colored folks who got burned out of their homes, or who ended up dead in the river, like fourteen-year-old Emmett Till. Yes, you took it all in, and learned to swallow the words that might land you hanging from a tree, your neck in a noose, and the crows picking at your beaten, bloody, half-burned body. You took it all in, and you learned what to do to keep on living.

In those days, our battles with Dr. King urging us forward on fields of honor, at Montgomery and Selma and Nashville, were yet to come. Those battles to open up bathrooms, water fountains, swimming pools, bus seats, restaurants, movies, train cars, public schools, and colleges. Those battles that would get us voting rights, marriage rights, and Miranda rights were yet on the horizon. And until that time, you walked in Jim Crow's shadow. To the beat of his drum.

1. Chilhowee Park

As a child, I adored Chilhowee Park. Located on the east side of Knoxville, it combined an amusement park, a zoo, a coliseum, a skating rink, and grounds for picnics and fairs. Going to Chilhowee meant glorious summertime was here, meant Mama would buy me mustardy dip dogs on a stick, blue raspberry snow cones, and, best of all, pink cotton candy that melted the moment my tongue touched it. The rides thrilled me though I dared not venture on the Tilt-A-Whirl because rides like that turned my equilibrium upside down and gave me an unbearable case of "the tickles"—butterflies on my stomach. I was especially taken with the Merry-Go-Round—all gaudy ornamentation, garish mirrors that sparkled in the sunlight, and huge pastel-painted horses. Mama would lift me up, sit me on the fake, painted saddle, then stand beside me so I wouldn't fall. Gripping the reins, I'd pretend I was a cowgirl hunting down outlaws, making sure justice was done. Along with the Ferris Wheel, that was my very favorite ride. After the rides, I looked forward to the wondrous sights awaiting me at the zoo. Where a regal-looking lion paced back and forth in his cage, and a slimy-looking alligator wiggle-waggled into swampy water; where chattering monkeys scampered across the trees, or hung upside down by their tails, and where humongous elephants showered themselves in water they blew out of their trunks. Chilhowee was my Disneyland. What more could I ask? Except maybe for fireworks.

One summer day, Mama and I were standing in line for one of the rides. She was holding my hand and I was holding a snow cone. I looked up and noticed a white banner draped on a fence. I must have been in kindergarten by then because I had begun to read signs aloud. Mama, ever the teacher, had taught me to sound out the syllables, and put them together. When I caught sight of the banner, I, automatically, began to sound out the words.

"Jul... July... four... th... July fourth," I read. Having gotten through the first two words, I started on the next word. It was a long one. "Cel... cela... brey... shun. Celebration."

I paused to take a bite of my icy, sweet snow cone before I went back to work. "Come... see the... fy... fire... wu... works. Fireworks." I had been so busy sounding out the words that I hadn't really taken in their meaning. Until now. It took only seconds for the message to sink in. They were going to have fireworks! Oh, boy! Oh, boy! I started to jump up and down, jerking Mama's hand. "Mama, Mama, can we come to the fireworks? Please? Pu-leese?" I pointed at the banner.

Mama looked down at me, smiling, and then up at where I was pointing. As she read the sign, I saw her face change. Not all at once, gradually. It was sort of like watching vanilla ice cream melting down. She blew out a breath and hunkered down beside me, still holding my hand, her black hair shining in the sun. "Honey, we can't come." Her voice cracked, like something was in her throat, and her dark brown eyes had turned into storm clouds.

I didn't understand what was wrong. "Why?" I whined, getting ready to bawl my eyes out.

"We can't come," she answered me, "because they don't allow Colored people to come to the park on the fourth of July. Only White people can come."

My heart plunged to my toes. "Only White people?" I asked. I knew already who *they* were and I knew already that they didn't want us in places where they went unless we were there to work for them. I felt a sob hitching in my throat.

Mama tried to make it up to me by saying, "We can come to the park on August eighth because that's our holiday. The day we got word Mr. Lincoln had freed us." She stopped and silence hung heavily as if the whole world had stopped with her. Stopped and gone silent.

I wondered how we could be free if I couldn't come to see fireworks on the fourth of July? And why was their freedom day different from ours? But I didn't say any of that; I just stood there holding Mama's hand.

At last, she spoke again: "Maybe there'll be fireworks then." She tried to put a wistful, little smile on her lips as she added, "And anyway, who cares about the fourth of July? We can come to the park any Thursday we want, all summer long."

Her voice tried to convince me that it didn't matter, but her tone didn't match her eyes. They were very dark, flat, and unreadable. I think she was angry, though, because she was squeezing my hand so tightly that I thought my fingers would break. She finally let go when she stepped up to the ticket booth for the Ferris Wheel.

I wanted to cry with disappointment, but I didn't want to be a baby out here at the park, so I sniffed back the tears. While Mama was paying for the tickets, I took a big swallow of my blue raspberry ice cone and gagged. It tasted different now. Like I'd swallowed something gone-over spoiled. Something old and maggoty. I deliberately let the cone I was holding fall to the ground because I could suddenly hear the loud rumble of mustardy dip dog, sweet cotton candy, and raspberry ice churning wildly in my stomach. Before I could help myself, my special, summertime treats gushed up from my belly like a geyser, and as I bent over, throwing up on my new Mary Janes, my eyes caught sight of the bright blue, raspberry ice spilling out of its red cup on the painted, white, concrete steps.

2. Uptown on Gay Street

In Knoxville, you did your shopping and banking uptown on Gay Street. No shopping centers dotted the landscape then. It was on Gay Street that I saw White people—driving their Buicks or Chevrolets, hurrying along on sidewalks, waiting on customers in stores and in banks. That was the only time I did see them, except on television, or in the movies since ole Jim required us to live worlds apart. There were some stores uptown where Colored folks couldn't or, more accurately, wouldn't shop. Those were the places, the grapevine said, where the White saleswomen deliberately turned their heads when Colored folks walked in—places where they wouldn't let you try on a hat because White women wouldn't try on any item, much less buy it, if that item had touched the scalp or skin of the Coloreds. Those were the places Mama wouldn't step foot in. She kept to the big department stores like Miller's. You could try on hats there, but not "intimate" apparel, which meant lingerie. We knew that and we didn't embarrass ourselves by asking to try on bras or girdles. We just bought and hoped the item fit.

One day, when I was in junior high, I walked into Miller's hunting for a swimsuit. I'd saved some money, and was feeling independent and grown up, so I figured I'd get rid of the baby blue suit Mama had bought me and buy one myself. Inside the store, I made a beeline to the rack, hoping to find a Jansen suit. I had a passion for black at that point in my life. I thought that wearing black made you genuinely sophisticated and worldly, and I particularly liked the Jansen line. Their suits were a little pricey, but I thought they made you look slender and stacked. So, I'd made up my mind that I just had to have one. I went through two racks before I spied one hiding among an array of rainbow colors.

Breathless, I snatched it up and checked the tag for size and price. Relieved that I could afford it, and glowing with satisfaction that I was finally going to get the swimsuit I'd always dreamed about, I hurried over, without thinking about it, to the redheaded saleswoman who had been watching me and the half-dozen other Colored folks milling about. I knew she'd been watching. They always watched, waiting for us to steal something. And although I resented it—we all resented it—that day, I was too excited about finding the black Jansen to pay her much mind.

"I want to try this on. Please?" I asked her, holding the suit up. You always had to ask permission to try on clothes. If you didn't they'd call the manager. Then you'd have a nasty little scene.

The redhead was tall with a thin, long nose. She peered down at me over it, as if she smelled something funky. "You can't. Y'all know that," she said imperiously, in Tennessee twang,

"Huh?" I couldn't manage more than that. It wasn't unusual for me to get all tongue-tied with White folks. I always had a tough time remembering just what you were supposed to say to them, and how you were supposed to say it even though I had been well-trained by my parents and other grown Black folks in survival protocol. It was axiomatic that you say very little, or better still, nothing at all to White people unless you had to.

Redhead was turning away from me. I looked at the suit in my hand and remembered another one of the rules of Jim Crow living: You never, ever question White folks. Normally, I wouldn't, but this time, I said: "M'am, I want to buy this but I need to try it on first. Why can't I?"

She looked back at me over her shoulder. "Don't be stupid, girl. Ya know we can't let y'all try on swimmin suits. Y'all soil em."

As soon as the words were out of her mouth, I realized my mistake. But my reaction was strange. My feet felt like they were on fire. I started to look down to see if someone had put a burning match to them. But before I could, a sheet of flame encased my legs, raced up through my stomach, blasted into my chest, and finally surged into my ears. *Fire. I'm on fire*, I thought, blinking away hot tears. Yet, there were no flames that I could see. I looked up to see the redhead's mouth still working, saying something more, but I couldn't hear a word; it was like I had gone deaf or something.

Out of the corner of my eye, I saw one of my Sunday school teachers, Mrs. George, browsing through the racks nearby. I turned my gaze to her. She had obviously been listening to the exchange. She just stared at me, standing as still as a pillar of salt, her gloved hand frozen above the clothing rack she had been looking through. Her eyes held me; that's what I remember most about that moment—her eyes. They were deep, dark wells of sorrow. And they made me want to cry, or shriek, or tear somebody's throat out. I had to look away.

Then, I remembered the suit. It was still in my hand. I looked at it and dropped it to the floor. I think I stepped on it as I stumbled away. After that, I, somehow, never liked the look of Jansen swimsuits.

Today, Jim Crow's rule of the day stretches far away in time's telescope—stretches back so far that sometimes it all seems a nightmarish dream. Nevertheless, it *was* real. Some say we should forget the past. Erase it. Move on. I disagree. Although it might be painful, looking back at the past is a good thing to do. There is history there. History that is real. Not touchy-feely fantasy that makes everybody look good for the camera.

Real history *is* my story. One that needs to be told. And *I* tell it because *you* can't. Because you shouldn't. You can *never* tell my story; you can *only* tell yours. But here's the important thing: If I tell mine and you tell yours, we learn from each other what it was like. We learn how we came through the good and the bad, how we survived in the face of overwhelming odds.

True history teaches you valuable things. When we tell our history, our stories show us who we are, where we belong, and where we came from. Our history, our stories can never put us to shame. They give us the gift of truth. And truth is a path that will bring us together.

Breaking the Rules

Miss Fannie Clay, Austin High's dean of students, glared at Nikki and me from behind the desk. It was ten o'clock in the morning and we were already in *deeeep* trouble.

"We don't," Miss Clay drawled, "allow our students to dress like juvenile delinquents." The students had dubbed her "The Whistler" because she made these awful whistling sounds when she pronounced certain words. As she talked, we'd roll our eyes or giggle behind our hands, and when we wanted a good laugh, some student would mimic her and everybody would fall out. We thought she was a joke.

But she's no joke today, I thought as I took a peep at Nikki from behind my sunglasses. Nikki looked like Nikki Giovanni always looked: Self-confident, gutsy, and ready to sweet-talk you into seeing things her way. A ghost of a smile danced around her lips. I wondered how she could be so cool, calm, and collected. Myself, I felt like something that was about to be shredded.

A half hour ago, the look on Miss Delaney's face, while she'd read the note Miss Clay had sent into our English class, told us we were headed for the shredder. It was one of those looks that parents, church ladies, and teachers give you when you've thoroughly messed up and they're about to wash their hands of you. Miss Delaney had given us that look, then said that we were to go to the dean's office immediately. Embarrassed, we'd gotten up and gathered our books as our classmates gaped at us in surprise. On the way out, I glanced over at Nancy and Brenda; their faces said, in no uncertain terms, that we were going to the gallows. Which was not surprising because, after all, well-behaved students didn't get called into The Dungeon of Death—the name I'd given Miss Clay's office. Truants did. And incorrigibles. But not honor roll students like us.

Why, I wondered, standing in front of Miss Clay, had I gotten myself into this? Mama was going to kill me. And Daddy...*Jesus!* Had any of the teachers told him yet? It wouldn't be long, I knew, what with him being right down the hall in the gym. Only a few weeks ago, as he was coming out of the boys locker room, Daddy had stopped me before I'd turned to go into Mrs. Jackson's health class.

He'd said: "Don't let Giovanni get you in trouble."

Since all this had been her idea, I guess you could say she had. It all started one evening when we were on the phone after she told me all the cool things she'd found out when she'd read up on the beatniks. It was dazzling to me how she was always presenting me with a new angle on the world. How she'd pull an idea out of her hat, and, *Presto!*, there'd be a new idea to consider that I'd never thought about before. She saw things in a way I found strangely compelling. Exotic almost. So different from the same old Knoxville point of view. I guess Daddy had picked up on that—the way I responded to Nikki's point of view. So when he'd said that about Nikki, I'd been surprised. Cautioning me about somebody or something was Mama's territory. Not Daddy's. And I'd thought: *Trouble?*

What possible trouble could I get in? I mean, what did he know anyhow? He was just an adult trying to cramp my style. So I didn't pay him any mind. I kept listening to Nikki. Now here I was. Course it wasn't all her fault. She didn't have to twist my arm, to tell the truth.

"I'm disappointed in you girls," Miss Clay said.

I studied Miss Clay's gray curls piled atop her head in an upsweep, her drab, charcoal, two-piece suit, her missing face powder and lipstick. Although I couldn't see her feet under the desk, I knew she had on her usual lace-up, black, granny shoes and heavy, cotton stockings, the kind Auntie always wore.

We, on the other hand, were dressed like the people we called ourselves championing: The beatniks. We were outfitted in all black because, Nikki had said, the beats always wore black; we were wearing oversized, pullover sweaters, short skirts that we'd had to roll at the waist to get them short enough and long black socks that we'd pulled up to look like we had on tights. To top things off, our heads were covered with black scarves arranged in the beat style, and we were sporting the most essential item of all—black, wraparound sunglasses. My heart was hammering at triple speed. We'd racked up a bunch of dress violations with our outfits. Especially the short skirts.

Miss Clay gave our outfits a nasty, once-over look. "Take off those sunglasses!" She barked. After we did, she asked: "What do you have to say for yourselves?"

I went stone mute. We'd defied the rules. Deliberately. For a good cause, of course. Undoing injustice was the reason, but would she understand? As I looked at Miss Clay's outfit once more, something occurred to me that I hadn't really paid attention to before, something I hadn't realized before. And that, in a nutshell, was: The way you dressed and wore your hair was a badge of respect for the order of things, a signal that you conformed to the traditions of the times. That's what Miss Clay's outfit said. That she conformed to tradition. That she had respect for the order of things as they stood. What Nikki and I had on said that we were outside the pale, as it were. That we were non-conformists, outlaws, or, worse, rebels, and tradition could just go to hell as far as we were concerned. This was not a message respectable, Negro high school girls were expected to send. I wondered if Nikki had realized that.

"Well?" Miss Clay drawled. "Do you have anything to say? I'm waiting."

Nikki, I knew, could handle this better than me. I kept mum, and glanced at her. She looked delighted at the open invitation to argue our case and opened her mouth to do it. It was a matter of righting wrongs, standing up for the underdog, she began. We wanted to dress like the beatniks in order to protest the unfair way they were being treated. It was wrong for people to think they were a bunch of nuts only because they dressed in bohemian style, Nikki said. Why should they get a bad reputation because they had different values and marched to a different drummer? It was unfair to make them outcasts, or brand them as criminals. It was just wrong. And we wanted to stand with them in solidarity.

Solidarity. That Nikki could really talk shit. You could always count on her to bring in some shiny, new words, and put them on the table. I was pleased to pick that one up, and I put it aside for future use. For a few more minutes, she laid it out, like a defense lawyer before the judge and I relaxed because it seemed to be going well. But then Miss Clay's expression suddenly went from unreadable to sourpuss. That was a bad sign. I had counted on Nikki being able to get us out of whatever trouble we'd be looking at for doing this since she could talk smooth-as-silk to adults. She almost always could slip out of any hot water she'd gotten herself into.

Suddenly, Miss Clay cut off the argument for our defense with an impatient wave. "Nikki, all that about the beatniks is just claptrap! You two just wanted to see if you could get away with this—this rebellious act!"

Nikki looked surprised at that. I guess she was. People mostly gave her the benefit of the doubt and heard her out, even if she sounded wacky to them.

After she'd made her accusation, Miss Clay, sat back in the chair, clasped her fingers over her chest, closed her eyes, and said nothing for what seemed like eternity. Nikki turned to me, lifting her shoulders in a shrug, and rolling her eyes. I let out a long sigh, shifting my weight from one foot to the other. Sweat gathered on my scalp.

Finally, Miss Clay opened her eyes. *It's all over,* I thought, feeling like Alice facing the Red Queen. *It's off with our heads!*

"You girls flagrantly broke the rules. Suspension is the punishment for that." She paused and looked pointedly, first, at Nikki, then at me.

Suspended? What's Mama gonna say? And Daddy? Suspension was major disgrace. I couldn't get suspended! I'd never live it down! My parents would never live it down! I never thought we'd get in this kind of trouble! My face flooded with shame. I clasped my hands behind my back to control their shaking. Nikki opened her mouth to say something, but Miss Clay glared at her to be silent. For once, thank God, Nikki held back.

When she saw that she wouldn't be interrupted, Miss Clay said: "What I'm going to do is send you both home to change your clothes instead of suspending you. I'm calling your mother, Frankie, over at Vine Junior. You go straight to her. Nikki, I'll be phoning Mrs. Watson, too..."

As she went on, I took a deep breath and silently thanked the Lord. *I musta been crazy to do this!* I scolded myself. *Why did I think I was gonna get away with it without Daddy and Mama finding out?* I was quaking inside because I knew, for sure, that I was up to my neck in trouble, now. My mother, being a stickler for keeping to the rules, was not going to like what I'd done. And she wouldn't hesitate to show me how much. I was too old for spankings, but she could be creative with punishments, I'd learned in the past. *Maybe she'll boil me in oil, or sentence me to be tarred and feathered,* I thought to myself as a joke. But it wasn't going to be funny, I knew. Not when Mama got through with me.

Miss Clay went on, "... you must be dressed correctly before you come back to school. No scarves, no sunglasses, no short skirts. And make sure you come back today before the end of lunch. Any questions?" We shook our heads like deaf mutes. "Then you are dismissed."

In the hall, Nikki and I tried to shore each other up. At least, she tried to comfort me because I was plainly panic-stricken, knowing the worst was yet to come. Nikki waved and gave me a little smile as she went out to the bus stop; I made tracks across the street to my mother's school. As I walked, dread settled on me like a thousand hornets.

Rounding the gymnasium corner at Vine Junior, I could see Mama in profile, sitting in her tiny office. I stopped for a moment, trying to figure out what I could say, how I could tell her what I'd done. She was looking down at her desk, probably grading papers. I could see her medium-length, black hair parted on the side, styled in the page boy she always wore, lipstick almost shockingly red against her fair skin. The gym clothes she wore—crisp, white shorts, shirt, and socks with white tennis shoes—made her look neat, almost prim, not casual or sporty. She set an example because she insisted that her students start out clean and neat for gym even though they'd get sweaty playing ball or exercising. That was Mama. Always insisting you walk the straight and narrow. And you'd better walk it looking the proper way. Her students seemed to love her. With them, she was firm, no-nonsense, and even-tempered. Adults and her friends mostly said that she never lost her temper, and always smiled. *Such a lady and so nice,* they'd say. Far as I was concerned, they just didn't know. She could roar like a tiger without ever raising her voice. Have you quaking in your shoes with just one look.

Now, she glanced up and beckoned me into her office. There was a stern look on her face as she looked me up and down. "So that's what you had on at school. No wonder Miss Clay was upset." Mama's voice was icicles.

Even though I knew Miss Clay would be true to her word and tell on me, I was amazed that Mama had already found out. I'd only just left Austin about five minutes ago. There was no phone in Mama's office, none in Vine Jr. except in the principal's office. *How did Mama find out so fast?* I asked myself. *How did adults always find out so fast what you'd been doing?* I concluded either they had telepathy or the fastest, most efficient grapevine ever known to man.

I opened my mouth to defend myself, but Mama anticipated me. She held her hand up like a cop stopping traffic and shut me up before I could start. "I won't ask you why you did it right now. We can talk about that tonight at home. Miss Clay says you're to change and get back to school right away." Rankled and tight-mouthed, she looked at her watch. "Good thing this is my break period since I'll have to take time out to drive you home."

"No you won't, Mama," I said, taking off the scarf and sunglasses, then unrolling my skirt so that it was normal length at mid-calf. I pulled the oversized black sweater over my head, revealing the blue blouse I was wearing underneath. The black socks I folded down to my ankles, the way I usually wore them. When I finished, I stood there, waiting for the axe to fall.

She nodded that the transformation was acceptable. "That's the way you looked when you left the house this morning. I wondered how you'd managed to change your appearance. You must have changed in the bathroom." Pushing aside the papers she'd been grading, Mama swiveled around in her chair. "Sit down," she said, pointing to the chair against the wall.

I did as she told me, bracing myself for what was to come. My hands were knotted into sweaty little fists. Looking like a hanging judge, Mama's face was a study in displeasure. "I don't like what you did. You know better than to go over the line. Rules are there for a reason. You don't just take into your head to ignore them, or defy them."

I saw an opening and decided to plead my case. "But Mama, it was for a good cause. Besides, Reverend King said sometimes you ought to break the rules. Like what Rosa Parks did when she broke the rules down there in Alabama. When they're unfair, you should do something to show people the injustice, right?"

Mama stared at me silently. Her eyes were dark and serious looking. She pursed her lips, thinking. Then she said, "First of all, I know my daughter. You had other reasons for what you did, didn't you?"

My eyes went to the floor and I nodded. Busted. She was right. The beatniks took a back seat to the plain, ole fact that I wanted to do something outrageous. Something so people would see me, Frankie, instead of seeing Coach and Estelle's daughter. I wanted my own identity. Even though I was realizing that what I'd done hadn't turned out to be the best way to get it.

"Second," Mama went on, once I'd nodded, "you've got to understand something, Frankie. Breaking rules is not something you do without expecting serious consequences. What Rosa Parks did was a courageous act. What Negroes are doing all over the South to show how unfair segregation is, that's a very ethical, moral thing to do. But..." Mama hesitated for a few beats.

Uh, oh, I thought, *when she says "but" like that, it's all over for me.*

"...you cannot compare what you did today with the Civil Rights Movement that's taking place. You and Nikki were being rebellious. Not moral. Be honest enough to admit that." She paused.

I felt my face flush at her challenge. Before I could figure out what to say, she went on. "This is your punishment. First, you're going to apologize to Miss Clay for doing this. Second, you will not be receiving or making phone calls for one month."

I gasped and my mouth fell open.

"Third, you'll be grounded for one month. While you are grounded, your friends can't come over." She kept going, but it was too painful to keep listening.

Bad enough to be grounded, stuck in the house without friends, car rides, or parties. But kissing my telephone privileges goodbye for that long! I felt like she'd delivered a mortal wound that I'd never recover from. What would I do without the telephone? I wouldn't know what was going on. I'd be like an outcast! Tears threatened to fall, but I swallowed them.

Mama continued, "You will only go to school and to church. No where else." She finally stopped doling out my sentence, and said: "I can see from the expression on your face that you didn't expect to pay the piper for breaking the rules. At least, not such a high price."

She was right. I'd thought maybe I'd lose my privileges for a couple of weeks. But not a month. "Mama, it's not fair to get punished for this. Why does everybody have to be the same? Why am I getting punished for dressing different? Why can't people let you be different?"

"Frankie, when I was young,..." Mama's voice had dropped low. Then she stopped completely, and looked out the window toward the field in back of the school where students played softball. She was silent for a while. It was like she'd forgotten what she was saying and had drifted off somewhere in time. I waited, staring at her.

Finally, with a start, she pulled herself back from wherever she'd been and began again. "When I was young, I did something that broke the rules, Frankie. And I paid a dear price for it. A very dear price."

Her eyes looked funny. Almost like she was ready to cry. That got my curiosity up. I leaned forward. "What, Mama? What happened?"

She dragged herself out of whatever she was remembering, and said: "Never mind what happened. Just listen to what I'm telling you." She came over to me, put her hand under my chin, and lifted it so that she could look into my eyes. "You have to learn that it costs to break the rules," Mama told me in a gentle tone. "Be sure you're ready to pay the price if you do."

Though I didn't know it then, there was more than a bit of irony in the fact that I'd gotten punished for wearing clothes that went against tradition. For looking like a rebel. It was ironic that in less than ten years, the hippies would be lambasted for the same thing. And Black people who chose to wear Afros would be roundly condemned. Tradition was about to get turned on its head. Though I didn't know it that day.

By the time I got back to Austin, I'd made up my mind to start writing a play about people making unfair judgments about others, about condemning people because they looked different, about the beatniks being outcasts because they'd broken the rules when they decided not to fit in. When I saw Nikki back to school, looking down in the mouth after her grandmother got through with her, I cheered her up by telling her about the play I was going to write. She thought it was a fine idea. Weeks later, the play, called *Julie and the Beatniks* was finished, and Nikki, having appointed herself my agent, proceeded, in Nikki-fashion, to talk our Sociology teacher into presenting it at school assembly as a class project.

But that's another story, another adventure I had back while Eisenhower was President, Ray Charles was singing "What'd I Say," and Nikki Giovanni was back in town.

Part Two: Baptism

Bloomington, Indiana and Evansville, Indiana

I know well what I am fleeing from, but not what I am in search of.

Michel de Montaigne

If you don't get lost, there's a good chance you may never be found.

Unknown

Baptism

It was a time when the old equilibrium capsized in the face of tidal change. It was a time when the bedrock of our lives, the order of the universe began to crumble. It was a decade that led us to the edge of chaos and left us hanging, about to slip, into the fearful darkness below.

It was the 1960's. Atlas shrugged and the earth proceeded to fly off its axis. Taboos tottered and fell. Comforting symbols—the ones we had used to draw certain conclusions flattering to the national ego—blew away as so much dust in the wind. Venerated idols scurried for shelter, sensing that they, too, had suddenly become vulnerable, expendable. The harbors of refuge we had depended on were not, we discovered, so safe and secure after all.

Time had caught up with and passed us. It was a new day. This decade of crisis and drama would take us to the water to be baptized: In fire and in ice.

From the beginning, lightning-like changes bombarded us and it became apparent, as the clock ticked on, that these changes would be too numerous for the brain to tally up each day. Reality became a kaleidoscope gone breathtakingly wild—the shock of it all leaving us bewildered, panting for respite, and grotesquely unprepared to cope.

Women, now unshackled by the pill, began to demand all manner of unreasonable things, dismissing the traditional role they had been assigned. Teenagers turned into ungrateful troublemakers, rejecting and condemning the lifestyles and values we had bequeathed them. Colored people forgot their place, stopped appealing for their civil rights, and started demanding something called Black Power, while insisting that the words "Colored" and "Negro" be dropped from the national vocabulary, in favor of the word "Black."

The world curved in on itself, shrinking from a vast globe, where people had previously been separated from each other by great distances, to a microcosmic community where people and nations were suddenly, instantly accessible to each other.

Pictures of the agonizing war in Southeast Asia now became a mere flick of a television switch away, thanks to a new roving space satellite. The rich and famous showed us that traveling to faraway places were only a trifling hop, skip, and jump from our own backyards. The great American dream machine, the automobile, macho symbol of American power and technology, leaped forward to take us from the Atlantic to the Pacific via new interstate highways.

Yesterday became a thousand years past and today catapulted us into galaxies far removed from our provincial imaginings. John Glen took off for a little jaunt around the earth in 1962. Six years later, television let us see the men of Apollo standing on moon soil. The first heart transplant got rave headlines. Computers were born. Data processing took its first curtain call, confident it would become the darling of world gone information crazy.

Like a fairy tale come true, America's standard of living flourished with the wave of a wand. A color television set could be had with the magic of easy credit. Fast food restaurants popped up like lilies of the field. Dishwashers, power lawn mowers, stereos, no-iron fabrics, shopping centers, frozen food, electric typewriters, and a myriad of other items for our convenience and self-indulgence appeared to bewitch and enchant us. Conspicuous consumption was on the rise thanks to the sorcerers of Madison Avenue who were more than happy to tempt us with their fairyland wares. After all, we were living in the land of opportunity, where you buy baubles and bangles to your heart's content, and where you're always in a dead heat to keep up with the Joneses.

In Knoxville, Tennessee, on January 11 of 1960, my mother staged a sweet sixteen birthday party for me. I have a black and white photo of that momentous occasion. Seven of my girlfriends and I are decked out in party hats and dressed in full regalia. Our faces are blithely innocuous, complacent, self-indulgent. Our eyes are as shiny as our smiles. You can fairly see by our expressions the bright horizons, the silver-lined clouds, and the sugarplums of future success just dancing in our feather-fluffed heads. In short, we were sailing high without a thought of possible storm clouds—full of confidence that no one would dare stick a pin in our fantasy-filled dreams.

I was mostly concerned that January, and in the ensuing months of my junior and senior years, with what I thought was essential to maintaining my membership in the status quo—that is to say, my peer group, to whom I genuflected at least twice a day. Essential, of course, meant a driver's license, and permission to wheel around in my father's Pontiac; privileges to use the family telephone which I outrageously abused; knowing how to do the latest dance; securing a place on the cheerleading squad; having a date for those all-important social rituals; and staying out as late as I could manage without being grounded for flagrant disregard of house rules.

My prime concern was what was taking place inside my insulated universe. But outside of it, forces were shaping up, swirling furiously, forming a tempest that would crack open my complacent insularity, and draw me into the vortex of its absorbing power. So while my high school salad days swiftly drew to a close in the spring of 1961, portents shot up to the heavens signaling the beginning of volcanic eruptions. Black college students had stormed and overrun ole Jim Crow's fort with their lunch counter sit-ins; soon, those same students would become the Freedom Riders, climbing aboard buses heading to Virginia, the Carolinas, Georgia, Alabama, and Mississippi to integrate the waiting rooms, bathrooms, and food counters in bus stations. To pay a bloody dues and call in long-standing debts. And quickly after that, acting on their faith in The Constitution and The Bill of Rights, young Black students and their White compatriots would put life and limb on the line down south by starting the Voter Education Project. Some paid, we know, with their very lives and never came home again.

Because of them, because of what they did, I came home from my freshman year of college to be greeted by the absence of "White Only" signs over water fountains, and bathrooms. Jim Crow, who'd guarded the bastion of White Supremacy for so long, no longer stood sentry, guarding greasy, five and dime food counters, Greyhound bus seats, hotel rooms, restaurants, public swimming pools, movie houses, or bowling alleys. The guardian had disappeared and I knew that a price had been paid in agony and in irretrievable loss. In a way, I felt guilty for I was reaping a harvest sown by others under soul-breaking circumstances, and I had done nothing: Some day, I sensed uneasily, time would catch up with me and, ready or not, it would be my turn. At the back of my mind, a question bumped insistently: When would a bill come due for me? And could I pay it with courage as these had?

In 1963, I was caught up by the tempest. George Wallace, who declared his intentions in his governor's inaugural speech—to preserve segregation that day, the next, and forever—set the tone. It was a bloody year. Blacks had made the historic choice to put their heads under the velvet-red hammer of the South. Violence whipped through the land like a whirlwind, bowing us down under the weight of its fury. That spring, the nation recoiled in horror at the news wire photos of Black people in Birmingham being chewed by police dogs and pounded by the stinging force of fire hoses. So when Dr. King vanished into the labyrinths of a Birmingham jail, we steeled ourselves for the worse while the federal government shuddered at the thought of his very possible demise. In June, Medgar Evers was shot down like a dog in front of his wife and children—shot in the back by assassins who lacked the manhood to look in his eyes as they delivered the contract that robbed him of his life. Yes. It was a bloody year. And America shook its collective head in regret as Walter Cronkite continued to wax lyrical on the evening news about the awful things happening to America. But there was more to come.

In August of 1963, Dr. King and his legion of followers marched on Washington to ask the best of this nation. It was a golden moment, an oasis of hope in a desert of impending despair, a proud moment worthy of the time in which it occurred: August, a word meaning "that which inspires awe, that which is imposing, dignified, majestic; something elegant and correct." At that moment, King's voice became a shooting star blazing the heavens; his words daring us to mate belief and vision—challenging us to mate brave quests with bold deeds. He was magnificent.

But we were not. We were unequal to the task he put before us. We would not trust in a thing long packed away like the toys of childhood—our common humanity. And so it began

Slaughter of the lambs. September, 1963. Fifteen sticks of dynamite blew promise to the winds and four Black children to bits one Sunday morning at the 16th Street Baptist Church in Birmingham. The bomb had been deliberately timed to go off during Sunday school when children would be present. Incredulous, I reeled at the abomination, unable to grasp, at first, that White people could hate us with such vengeance. Then, time swooped down like a hawk and dug its razor talons into the top of my head. It was the first time I tasted rage. The first time I ached for bloody revenge.

The first assassination. November, 1963. When Atlas shrugged, I felt the staggering shock of disorientation as the bullets of November smashed into President Kennedy's head. It was surreal. Unthinkable. I couldn't believe it. An American president murdered? It just didn't happen here. Not here. Not in America. But it had. And now the way I looked at the world had been turned upside down.

Uprisings and insurrections, 1964 to 1967. The devil's rain drummed down on the streets of America's ghettos. Zigzagging across the nation, the rain turned into a torrent unleashed, writing America's story in fire and in death. The festering sores of racism had burst open, seething with infected, venomous pus. Death, it seemed to me, was everywhere—racing like wild fire from Harlem, to Detroit, to Atlanta, to Los Angeles, fanning out to become a contagion. And the leprous face of this contagion was mine. And yours. Was ours.

Was America.

But none of us wanted to face up to its cause. *Not my fault!* We cried, having been brought to the rivers of Jordan. So we took to the hills, searching frantically for a hiding place where we would, nevermore, have to look in the mirror reflecting that diseased face. But hiding places are either temporary or illusory. (Most often, both.) And our hiding places could not shield us, for time was not going to let us off the hook.

1968. When the guns of April thundered, I was not at all surprised by the manner and circumstances of Dr. King's death. I only marveled that it had been so long in coming. For at some point—perhaps the day when he took an irreversible step, speaking out against Vietnam, and against economic oppression—at some point, I knew he would not be permitted to live. For me, it had been a matter of waiting, but hoping against hope that America would spare him, thereby, sparing the nation of another bloody stain of guilt on the book of records. But it was just too much to hope for, I suppose. He had dreamed too much, this dreamer. He had asked too much. He had asked and we had found ourselves wanting, found ourselves quite short of heaven. And that shamed us, frightened, and angered us. It repelled us and filled us with self-loathing. So we turned on the dreamer. We marked him as the cause of our awful torment. And the inevitable came to pass.

This decade of the 1960's had opened with the ringing voice of John F. Kennedy promising to usher in new frontiers of possibility and greatness for America. Camelot had shimmered on the horizon and, indeed, it seemed, then, that this might be the best of all possible nations. But Camelot had been blasted, over and over again, from the horizon. The summer of 1968 took the heart, finally, out of me. With Bobby Kennedy's slaughter, my faith in America's promise to deliver on its own ideals crumbled, like brittle, yellowed leaves. For I had seen him as the last chance, the alternative to the split between Black and White America. Maybe he would not have been a miracle worker, and perhaps my faith would have been replaced with disenchantment, disquiet, and cynicism. But we will never know. With his death, America was set on a course in deadly waters where treacherous currents shipwrecked our efforts to steer clear of the shoals.

By late summer, White America was offering up its own children as a sacrifice to the gods of greed and chaos. In August of 1968, courtesy of live television, I watched as the Democratic National Convention became a hideous parable of this decade. I saw, in living color and straight from the streets of Chicago, this nation and its institutions grappling desperately, grotesquely, fighting savagely to deny the reality of change. I watched, in paralyzing fear and anguish, as convention delegates, news people, young protesters, bystanders, and medics—all—were sacrificed at the altar of law and order by the nightsticks of the Chicago police swinging, smashing, crushing, beating heads in a relentlessly, bloody, military cleansing. I was appalled. It struck me, then, that a great, blind malevolence was stalking the land. That this nation had finally turned in on itself, and was beginning to eat at its own insides, at its own marrow, was beginning to feast on its own young.

By then, this watershed decade had transcribed, with a pen of blazing, chilling light, the best and worst of times on the soul of the young girl I had been.

Gone were the sugarplums that had danced in her head. Gone were the silver clouds that had lit up her eyes.

Innocence was no more.

She had been brought to the river. And baptized.

Fever

1. Green Eyes

As soon as I sat down beside her, Tweety Bird, squeaked, "Let's have a toast!" Her high-pitched voice had earned her the nickname when she was in elementary school and it stuck. Nobody called her Pat.

Motor-mouth Joann, as tall and skinny as Tweety was plump, jumped in, "Here's to us!"

"And to Christmas vacation!" Stacey added.

The four of us raised our glasses and I sent dagger thoughts at Stacey sitting across from me. *Where the hell had she been?* Her face was closed and there was a tightness around her mouth. Some people said Stacey looked like Lena Horne; others didn't see the resemblance because of Stacey's startling green eyes that just knocked you out when you looked directly into them. The effect, to me, was more pronounced because of the mole on the crest of her left eyebrow. It was like a punctuation mark, I sometimes thought, at other times, like a butterfly's wings.

We clinked our glasses and drank while I tried to catch Stacey's eye, but she and Joann had their heads together, giggling about something. That just served to stoke the coals of irritation simmering in my gut. Since we'd picked up Stacey at her dorm in Joann's ancient Plymouth up to now at the bar, I'd been maneuvering without success to get Stacey alone. To ask her what was up. Why she hadn't been in touch. Usually, she picked up on the signals I'd give her to go someplace where we could talk in private. Tonight, though, she acted like she was blind, deaf, and dumb to my cues. Frustrated, I took a deep breath through gritted teeth. Tweety bounced up, signaling me to watch her seat, and hopped away to another table.

I plopped my purse in her chair to let the empty-seat searchers know this one was taken. This was the last Saturday night before Christmas break and it looked like all the Black students at Indiana University were here and ready to do some serious partying. People were leaning against walls, standing two rows deep at the bar, squatting on every chair. The place was packed out.

Years ago, Black students had christened this place "The Hole." You got in by going down a flight of concrete steps that disappeared under the ground. Legend said the Black Legionnaires ran out of money after putting in the basement of what was going to be their American Legion Hall. Instead of giving the whole thing up, they made do and turned the underground basement into a bar. It wasn't much for looks—an old, wooden bar at one end of the room, three or four dozen rickety chairs and tables scattered round, a pot-belly stove sitting near the bathrooms for heat in winter, ceiling fans that pushed hot air around in summer, and the essential jukebox in the corner—no, not much for looks, but we didn't complain since it served as somewhere we could dance to the latest James Brown, Ray Charles, or Temptations records.

As I watched people milling around "Ho-ho-ho-ing" each other, my mood blackened. I stole a glance at Stacey, my mind racing. Two whole weeks. And not a word from her. What was wrong? Why hadn't she called? What was up? My stomach lurched, a sure sign that things were amiss.

Over the hum of voices, Little Willie John's silky-smooth voice drifted up and out of the jukebox, singing

"Fever," an ancient favorite of mine. The song's words were all about misery throbbing in your gut. Love misery. The kind that that settles into your bones. But it was really Little Willie John's voice—rough and smooth, like cayenne sprinkled on honey—that stitched the words into your soul. Stitched them, and then laced them with an aching so hot it boiled your blood. He shouted out a heat-soaked wail, and I turned up my glass to drink, glancing again at Stacey. The taste of scotch on my tongue was bitter and oily. Yeah, the man was singing about the love-fever: The kind that feels like blistering, summertime heat. The man was singin bout love-fever that has you searching for ice water to cool yourself down. His voice lit the fire of memory.

2. Heat

I caught the fever the first time I ever laid eyes on Stacey. That was a couple of weeks after I came to Indiana University. She was in The Commons, the noisiest place on campus, where students swarmed between classes to gobble down doughnuts and coffee. I liked to study there; the music was surprisingly good for a place that White folks managed, and I could smoke and sip coffee. Which I was just learning to drink. The cigarettes and coffee conspired to make me feel all grown up. But the truth was, I was scared shitless to be on a huge college campus where I didn't know anybody, where I was hundreds of miles away from home, and expected by the folks back there to make the kind of grades that would do them proud. On top of all that, I was literally surrounded, for the first time in my life, by more White people than you could shake a stick at. The truth was: I was a wreck.

That day I first saw Stacey, she was playing cards in The Commons, and I was between classes, sitting at a table alone. For some reason, I glanced up from reading about Odysseus fighting the one-eyed Cyclops, and that's when I saw Stacey gesture for me to come over. I was surprised, and thought she was motioning to someone else because we didn't know each other. Last week at a dance, somebody had pointed her out as a Greek and upperclassman. So I knew who she was, but I didn't think upperclassmen noticed freshmen. Feeling awkward and more than a bit flattered that she'd noticed me, I got up and tramped over to her table. Cigarette smoke curled around the heads of the four Bid Whist players, who studied their cards like they held the secrets of life. Two of the players were guys, signifying loudly as they slapped cards on the table with pleased exaggeration. That meant they were winning. Stacey—her auburn hair caught up in a ponytail—was doing some serious signifying herself. I was startled by the contrasting delicate curve of her neck and what was coming out of her mouth. She looked refined; her words were not. Obviously, she could handle herself and that impressed me.

I slid into a chair next to Stacey and stayed quiet. In between the card-slapping, she leaned over, smiling, and introduced herself. The moment she turned those dazzling green eyes on me, whatever else was going on in the place stopped and melted away. Though I tried not to gaze at her like an idiot, I found I could barely catch my breath. It was like one of those corny, Hollywood boy-meets-girl movies. Only this was girl-meets-girl. And, right then, I was lost. Lost. Or, maybe, found. Depends on how you look at it.

How I looked at it was this way. For a very long time, I'd known I didn't feel boys the way I did girls. In junior high, when other girls talked about liking boys, I'd used hook and crook to sidestep the subject. In a way, I was saved by Mama's rule of no dating until I finished ninth grade. But high school forced me to change my tactics. No more sidestepping. It was time for dates and boyfriends. Fear of being found out pushed me into conforming. So I made sure I got the boyfriends—Richard and Russell, to name two—and I blended in by dating Sammie, Merlton, Avon, and Bennell to keep up appearances. I even flirted a bit. Fear of the words, the accusations—*She's funny! She's a bulldagger! She's a dyke!*—fear of being severed, cut off from the pack, the crowd, the group taught me how to make myself fall in step, act in the conventional way, say the appropriate words. All in service of weaving an illusion, of building a camouflage so I wouldn't stand out as different. I blended in like a chameleon and the crowd bought my act.

It all went so well that I almost believed it myself. Almost. Until a willowy leg, a curve of hip, a swell of breast, or soft lips would bring to fore a distant longing in me, like tinkling bells from a far place. Like the smell of jasmine on evening wind. The ache inside me would start then—the ache to break free of the box I had put me in. Stacey's eyes that day I first met her—they were full of something that started that ache again. And I promptly slapped it down.

Black students at I. U. hung with other Blacks, so I saw Stacey a lot—at dances, at The Commons, in the cafeteria, between classes, at basketball and football games. Everywhere. By the time I was a sophomore, I had a serious ache, but I choked it off, never let it come up for air, hid it from myself in a secret vault, and buried the vault under boy-dates because I didn't want to admit the vault even existed. To do that I had to psych myself out. Not just act out the lie like I did in high school, but, this time, buy into and believe it.

Believing it was infinitely easier my junior year when something to do with family and finances kept Stacey at home the whole of what was supposed to be her senior year. That year, my pattern was set, and, had anyone bothered to notice, easy to predict. Always, I'd hook up with guys who were either engaged to the girl back home, or seniors on their way out, never to return. That I deliberately picked the unavailable ones, that my real motives were hidden deeper than the deep blue sea, never occurred to me because I'd buried the secrets in the vault under layers of double-dealings and deceit. And so, I went on living in Emerald City until the summer before my senior year when Stacey and I both ended up in summer school.

It had been muggy and humid-hot in Bloomington, so typical of Indiana summers. No air conditioning in the buildings. No ceiling fans. And the dorms were steaming. Girls moved about, in their rooms and down the halls, in panties and half-slips pulled up over bare breasts—the only way to cope with the weight of heat pressing down relentlessly. It made everybody edgy, the heat. You couldn't escape it. The television news added to the edgy feeling by telling us about the students pouring into Mississippi to register the Black people there as voters. They were calling it Mississippi Freedom Summer, and making, in their reports, fearful insinuations about White backlash. Everybody knew the reporters meant the Klan riding with their burning crosses. They'd torch a Black church in a minute—and do even worse. Seemed like everybody was living in the hot time.

The friends Stacey and I usually hung with weren't there, and my summer roommate was a no-show, so Stacey started coming to my room a lot. Because neither of us had much money, at first, we'd go to all the freebie campus theater productions and musical concerts together; sometimes, we made library dates to study together. Occasionally, we'd have dates with boys, not many though because the fraternity brothers we dated weren't around. Mostly, we laughed a lot. When she laughed, the mole above her eyebrow looked, for all the world, to me like a gorgeous butterfly. She'd always thought the mole made her look ugly. I told her that I thought it made her look beautiful and she was touched, her eyes filling so that they looked like the crystal green waters of the ocean.

As the days wore on, I realized the more I was around Stacey, the more I wanted to be around her. She was like a magnet, always pulling me toward her. And when I saw that, I tried to back off, not spend quite as much time with her. For a while, I'd purposely leave my room at the time she usually dropped by, or I wouldn't answer the phone, just in case she was calling. I did it because I knew what the pull was and I fought against letting it slip into my consciousness. Each time it loomed up, I'd mentally tiptoe around it, or I'd try to quietly leave it in a room by itself. When it wouldn't stay gone, I locked it into the bottom drawer of my mind. But it—the feelings—wouldn't stay behind the barricade. What I'd done before, I realized, wasn't working: Because Stacey was golden fire to me, both frightening and inflaming me. The fear kept me in check, but the fire—the fever—drew me. And this time, I couldn't shake the fever loose. This time, my body was telling me things in hot-breathed whispers, in burning night dreams that I couldn't, and wouldn't push away.

And so came the Sunday afternoon of July fourth weekend. It was so humid that sweat popped out on your skin the moment you stepped out of the shower. With heat this intense, the dorm was near empty. Most people were out somewhere trying to find a cool spot. I was in the first floor lounge, watching television when Stacey came through, looking for me. She sat as close to me as she could without causing raised eyebrows if somebody walked in. We didn't talk much, just sat there, watching yet not watching the black and white pictures marching across the screen. We sat. Breathing in and out, drinking in each other's nearness. It was as if everything had conspired to bring us to this moment. I can't remember how long we sat that way. An hour, maybe. Or, perhaps, just ten or fifteen minutes. It seemed as if we were suspended in time. Held fast by a raging fever that had a life of its own. One that was palpable in the summer air. One that was full of sparks, like a tinderbox ready to go up in flames.

Without speaking, Stacey took my hand and we both got up. There were a few girls in their rooms on the first floor; we could hear them as we went up the stairs to the second floor where my room was. We went up, like sleepwalkers. And, without words, into my room. Neither of us knew what we were doing that first time, but it didn't matter.

Tenderness. Love. Joy. Release. That was what mattered.

That time, and the next, and the next.

3. Perfect Fit

Suddenly, somebody at the next table shrieked with laughter. It pulled me out of memory lane and back to The Hole. To get my bearings, I looked around. Joann was standing by the entrance, struggling to make herself heard on the public phone. Stacey's seat was empty; in the milling crowd, it took a few seconds to find her standing on the dance floor, laughing it up with Gene. Tweety, back at our table, asked me if I wanted a beer. Since beer was my drink of last resort, and I still had some money for another scotch, I shook my head.

"Frankie," she said before she headed for the bar, "Cheer up. You're a cute girl, but you're chasing the guys away with the gloom and doom face. Smile some, girl!"

My glum mood answered her silently as I watched her go. *Smile about what?*

I couldn't shake the down-in-the-dumps, blue devils. To cap it off, somebody dropped a nickel and Ray Charles came up singing "Born to Lose." It was slow-drag time. On the floor, dancers draped themselves tightly around each other, hugging and clutching. Stacey, I saw, was dancing with Gene. One of his arms held her tightly at her shoulders, the other at her waist, his cheek pressing against her temple. Both of her arms were clasped around his back.

Perfect fit, I thought. *Dancing together, they're a perfect fit.*

Although I'd seen her dance with boys before, tonight, the sight of her body snuggled so close to Gene brought me close to tears. Why couldn't it be me out there with her? Why couldn't I nuzzle my face in her neck, fit my body close to hers, move slow and easy on the dance floor to Ray's heavy-hearted, country blues? The ache for Stacey was so clear and strong that I felt like running out on the floor, tearing her away from Gene, and screaming out our secret. Instead, I lowered my head to hide my face. Moments later, I saw an open palm under my nose and I lifted my eyes to Freddie's.

"Come on," he said, inviting me to join him on the floor.

Swallowing back the tears, I arranged a plastic smile on my lips and gave him my hand.

Put on the mask, girl, I told myself.

Out on the dance floor, my eyes searched for Stacey while I thought, once again, about the summer of 1964.

4. Secret Lives

For a few weeks, our secret life remained securely hidden. Then, there was that close call one afternoon in my room when Lynn, a student in one of my classes, barged in without knocking. Going by looks, nothing out of the ordinary was happening in that room, but if you went by gut feelings, the room was heavy with tingly, I-got-a-itch-for-you vibes. Stacey and I were sitting on the bottom bunk bed, books on our laps. Because my head was turned toward Stacey and away from the door, I didn't see Lynn coming in. But something in Stacey's expression scared me enough to make me jump to my feet, my book landing with a heavy thud on the floor.

It was a weird moment: Lynn at the door, wearing her usual dull-witted, sleepy look; Stacey seated on the bed with a startled, almost terrified expression, and me up and ready to take on whatever unknown bugaboo had darkened my door. When I saw it was only Lynn, my alarm drained away, and I asked her, with more roughness than I intended, what she wanted. As she told me, I noticed her dense expression changing. Into what? Curiosity? Slyness? While I hurriedly dug out my class notes for her, she stared, mouth half-opened, at me and then at Stacey. With guarded wariness, Stacey, I saw, was taking Lynn's measure herself. Everything seemed to be taking a long time, or, at least, it felt like forever before I found the notes and held them out to her. Lynn took them, nodding her thanks, and wearing a kind of smirking grin as she backed out of the room.

The door shut and I realized I couldn't breathe, was, in fact, holding my breath. I sucked in air as Stacey lit a cigarette.

"That," Stacey declared, "was way too close for comfort. We've got to be careful from now on. That girl was like a hound dog smelling a fresh trail."

I wrinkled my nose. "Lynn? She couldn't find her ass if you showed it to her in a mirror." I waved the idea away, moving close to Stacey again. "Does not play with a full deck, that one."

"No, baby!" Stacey snapped. "No. Pay attention. That one smelled our vibe. And we cannot afford to let that happen again." Stacey's voice had turned into an ice storm.

I still didn't see cause for alarm. "I don't think she suspected anything," I said, sitting again, putting my arms around her. "Lynn's too stupid to notice stuff like vibes."

"No!" She shook me off and drew back. "No! Don't do that! We'll get caught doing things like that!"

If the room had been feverish with steamy vibes before, now it was a below-zero blizzard. I backed off and got up, fumbling for my cigarettes. As usual, my hands trembled when I was scared. And Stacey's tone of voice had scared me. She'd never used it with me though I'd heard her use it before when she meant to cut somebody to the quick— slice em, dice em, and serve em up on a platter. She was known for her sharp tongue.

I could see Stacey trying to take a hold of herself and calm down. After a moment, she spoke. "Look, you're my girl, Frankie. But we're not like them. So let's don't act like *them*."

I was confused. What did she mean, let's don't act like them? Did she mean for me not to put my arms around her? Not to kiss her anymore? What was wrong with showing affection? And just who was them? "Who're you talking about Stacey?" I shot back, knowing the answer all along.

"You know. *Them*." Her voice was a cold wind. "Those freaks! Bulldaggers!"

The words made me flush with embarrassment; and, at the same time, I felt the sting of insult, of absolute put down. Why did she have to use those names? It was the same as calling us niggers. Or calling girls bitches. Anger rumbled in my chest, the kind that would usually goad me into starting an argument, but I didn't want to fight with Stacey. Besides, I could see she was already fighting, struggling with some invisible thing inside herself. A nerve at her temple moved up and down, throbbing. Her mouth was a tight slash. Whatever this thing was, it was a fearsome opponent. And it made her face ugly. Silence lay hard in the room, and I let it lay.

The thing to do right now, I told myself, *is keep quiet. Be cool.*

Stacey peered at me across the room. "I guess this is our first lover's quarrel, huh?"

I said nothing. Mostly because I didn't know what to say. Doubts about Stacey and me swirled round my head like fireflies. The undertone in Stacey's voice when she'd used the word *bulldaggers* was poisonous. Hateful. How could she feel that way about herself? About me? Anxiety wrapped its fingers around my heart, forcing me to take a long, hard drag on my cigarette. She was watching me, waiting for a reply. Still, I said nothing.

"Forgive me?"

I didn't want to make her madder, so I nodded, abandoning my feelings, ignoring my unease. I nodded because I was afraid to put my feelings into words. Afraid to pursue the threads of doubt setting up house in my head. Afraid of the doors doubt might open that couldn't be shut again. The meddling voice in my head was shouting a warning from a distance, but I turned the volume down on it. All the while, silently beating myself up for a coward. A chicken-hearted coward.

Our senior year, after that summer, started off badly. Lynn, the dumb bunny, had started rumors about me being a dyke. About me and any other females she saw in my company. Despite the rumors, we snuck around so we could be alone. It was hard because when we did manage it, desire radiated from us like a boiling desert, and we didn't have a place we could go to touch. To cool the fever.

And it got to be doubly hard because fear of being found out began running us. Just like those caged, white, lab rats in my Psychology class, running round and round on a wheel. Caught up on a course that was leading us into undiscovered country, we had no one to help us find our way. Nobody to talk to about where we were going. If only we could've talked to each other about what we were feeling. About what was happening between us.

But fear hung over us like a dark cloud, urging us into secrecy, and secrecy posted "No Talking" signs in our heads. The desire we felt was taboo. The feelings were taboo. So talking about it was taboo. If I tried, Stacey would make a shushing sign and cover my lips with her fingers. That bothered me, but I didn't want to do anything to make things harder for us, so I let it go.

September's Indian summer faded and I began to see Stacey struggling, more and more, with that invisible thing inside her. And I was afraid of it because I knew it had something to do with us. Sometimes she looked so hollow-eyed. So strained. I could see it was beating her down on the outside. But, Lord, what was it doing to her on the inside? Taunting her? Torturing her? Making her hate herself? What if, one day, she started to hate me, too?

I pushed the question away. Hard.

5. At the Cloister

Two months later when Stacey and I walked across the campus, half-hidden in the shadows of the fading, evening light, dread was biting at my heart. A chilly, winter wind brushed against my bare legs and played with the hem of my skirt as we crossed the wooded campus: Two Black girls hurrying along, heads hunched forward, coat collars up, hands pushed deep into our pockets for warmth.

Faraway from the residence dorms now, we were passing Franklin Hall and several deserted classroom buildings, their darkened windows looking, to me, like watching eyes. A stand of trees—maple, maybe some oak and walnut, still holding on to most of their golden, red, and brown leaves—was just ahead. Stacey, a few steps ahead of me, moved swiftly into them. This was a secluded area so thick with ornamental shrubs, bush, and timber that students had dubbed it "The Cloister," a place as famous as "Kinsey Hollow," the make-out spot at Trees Center. I followed her in, glancing around to see if we'd ended up in the middle of couples sprawled on every bench, desperate for a place to make out. But nobody was here. She'd timed this just right. The deserted benches reminded me that our school was set, within an hour, to play our rival, Purdue, in a special nighttime football game. I looked around. Secret and cozy. That's the way this place felt. Or would have if I didn't have a queasy stomach about this meeting. I'd had one since Stacey had found me.

When she'd tracked me down an hour ago at The Commons and beckoned me out, there was a cloud of tightness on her face. Something was wrong and whatever it was had changed her face in a way I couldn't read. I'd come out into the hallway, and she'd put her hand on my wrist, pulling me into a darkened corner. Her grip on my wrist was a vise.

"You're hurting me, Stacey," I'd told her, but it was like she didn't hear me.

A fierce whisper leaped out of her throat. "We have to talk," she said. "Come on." And she'd said nothing more.

Now, here we were and I tried to get ready for whatever was coming. Stacey was standing deep inside The Cloister, partly in shadow, arms wrapped around herself for warmth, her face turned up to the night. My eyes swept in her profile, and I felt that something I always felt when I looked at her—a starburst of warmth, a surge of something electric pulling me to her. That electric current drew me close to her side.

"Frankie," she began, turning toward me, her voice earnest, too earnest, and low, "I want you to hear me out before you say anything. Okay?" She lifted her right hand and gently touched my cheek.

Somehow, that gesture which usually comforted me didn't, and I looked at her mole, my butterfly, at the crest of her left eyebrow for some sign of what she was going to say. When she was puzzled, or troubled, the butterfly's wings would lift as if it were ready to fly away. They had lifted.

"You know since Jimmy left and went to California, people, I mean... guys are asking me... Well, shit! I'm just gonna say it." Now, she took a deep breath. "I know you don't want to hear it, but we don't go out with boys enough. And it looks bad to people like Lynn. Just gives them ammunition to start shit, like she did." Barely concealed panic filled her eyes and she rushed on without looking at me. "I can't keep doing this." Her fist hammered the air as she finished, puffing for breath like she'd just run the 220.

Anger, deep and raw, flashed out of me so fast that my voice shook. It took me by surprise. "Why do you care what people like Lynn say? She's nobody! What are you so scared of?"

Stacey looked at me like she'd never see me before. "Well, hell, aren't you scared people will find out about us?"

I had to admit I was and I nodded. But then I realized I was tired of fear running us and I wasn't so scared that I'd give Stacey up for it. Which came as a revelation. I hadn't recognized before that I felt that way.

Stacey was reassured by my admission. "Okay, then. We don't want anybody to find out, so we've got to look normal. I've got to start dating somebody steady. You, too."

"Stacey, what the hell is 'normal' anyway?" I resented the word she'd used. It disrespected us, hissed that we ought to hang our heads in shame, slink away in disgrace.

A smile played on her lips. "Frankie, this is no time to be pulling out one of your technical arguments." She reached out and cupped my chin in the palm of her hand. "You know what I mean. We'll be graduating soon, and things with us will be different. We just have to do this a little while."

A dull pain crept into my throat. I wanted to say no. I wanted to plead with her. Beg if I had to. Whatever it took to avoid the sea change that was coming on. Instead, I heard myself saying, "If you've made up your mind, what can I say?"

The words tasted like gone-over milk in my mouth. The thought of her spending time with somebody else roused jealousy from its sleeping cave and forced it out into the night.

What if she leaves you? That meddling voice of mine whispered. The question dropped into my heart like a stone and I hung my head.

Stacey saw it and, in a rare gesture, she caressed my face. Impulsively, I grabbed her hand and kissed her palm tenderly. This time, she didn't draw away like she usually did. Instead, she sighed softly and murmured, "We'll be together, Frankie. But we've got to be careful. You're my girl; you know that. Don't you?"

"Yeah," I whispered, lifting my eyes to hers. They were shadowy pools of water, dark as the night that surrounded us.

"Ned's practically knocking down my door for me to date him steady, you know?" She turned away from me and sat on a nearby bench, beckoning me to come sit beside her. "Why not? He's a good guy, Frankie. Considerate. What do you think?"

Ned. My insides pained at the thought. "You're gonna date Ned? The puppy dog? He practically pants at your feet every time he sees you." I came over to her and sat down.

Stacey giggled. "Yeah. He's kind of like that, no lie. But he's manageable."

I made a face. I wanted Stacey all to myself, but if she had to date somebody, I told myself, Ned was the best bet. He was harmless. Better him than a few others I'd seen hanging around her. Like Lobo, or Honeybear. Cool, cute, and classy, the both of them. The kind of guys that girls fell over themselves to date. Guys like Honeybear and Lobo made me nervous. Yeah, Ned was the best bet for Stacey. He was nowhere near the cool and classy league.

Stacey read the worry lines in my face. "Don't sweat. It'll work out okay, Frankie. You just be sure you don't let some guy get too close to you. Or I'll get jealous."

My heart started beating as fast as a hummingbird's wings when she said that. Could it be she *did* feel the same way about me as I did about her? I fished for her feelings indirectly. "Maybe I want you to be jealous," I teased, "to prove to me you care." I leaned close to her, intending to give her a kiss on the cheek, but, this time, she pulled back and away.

Her brow furrowed, and the butterfly wings lifted again. "Hey! Be careful. Somebody could come by." She looked around until she was satisfied nobody was lurking in the bushes. "Why should I prove it? You already know I care, Frankie."

But I didn't really, and that was the moment I knew I wanted a commitment from her. Wanted it desperately. But if I asked, she might laugh at me, or, worse, leave me. So I kept my mouth shut.

As we were walking home, the meddling voice tried to ask me something, but I smothered it, laughing at some joke Stacey was telling me. That was the night I started saying to myself that who Stacey dated didn't matter because things would turn out okay. That was the night I started telling myself that I should settle for what we had right now and that I could be happy later on.

Besides, I asked myself, *what did I want her to commit to?*

The answer came back so loud and clear that I couldn't deny hearing it: *To me,* the voice said unequivocally. *I want her to commit to me. Forever.*

6. Distant Thunder

Ray Charles howled one last time and the music ended. Back at my table, Freddie winked at me as I sat down. My mask was still firmly in place and I gave him a big grin, waving at his retreating back. Then I turned my attention to Stacey; she seemed preoccupied, staring into her drink, but I was determined, this time, to get some answers. Asking her straight out where she'd been wouldn't really sound weird if I kept my tone of voice light. Kept it playful.

"Stacey," I smiled, "where've you been keeping your butt for the last two weeks? I been tryin to catch you between classes cause I wanted to get you to quiz me for a test." The lie came out easily enough. I don't know what I expected her to answer: *My finals were kicking my ass...I've been pulling all-nighters in the library...My graduate professor laid a twenty page paper on us.* Something like that. But not what I got. Which was her looking at me with fear in those green eyes. Just for a moment, I saw it. Naked. Unmistakable. And then she did away with it. I blinked, startled, wondering if I'd imagined it. But I knew I hadn't. Before I could figure out what to say, Tweety pointed to the entrance.

"Hey," she chirped, "there's Ned."

At the entrance, Ned looked around; Jo lifted her hand and shouted, "Hey, Cuz, over here."

I could've snatched her bald. *Why did she have to go and do that?* Then I remembered that Joann and Ned were cousins.

I rolled my eyes and gritted my teeth. *Damn...Damn...Damn! Why'd he have to show up?* I knew he'd bring his raggedy-ass behind right over here when he saw Stacey. And, shit, we'd never get rid of him! Getting Stacey alone tonight was going to be almost impossible now.

I watched him make a beeline straight for our table. He was good looking enough with an open face the color of bronze. A friendly guy who wasn't stuck on himself, but it was all I could do to be polite to him when he pulled up a seat next to Stacey, looking like the big, brown Collie dog that he was. She'd been dating him steadily for the past year. Since after that time at The Cloister. He wasn't the only one she dated, but she was with him enough to keep me uneasy. Right now, he was whispering something in her ear and she was smiling like she was eating it up. I couldn't stand it. Jealousy gnawed at me with such ferociousness that I jumped up and headed for the jukebox.

I dropped some coins in and pushed some buttons. Martha and the Vandellas came up with that driving rhythm that speaks to your soul. I didn't want to dance so I pretended to look for more records to play. Tweety bounded up to dance with Gene. Somebody came by and got Joann. Then Ned pulled Stacey out on the floor. Everybody was having a ball, boogying back. That was the last thing I wanted to do. My mind was stumbling, tumbling from one thing to another: From the fear in Stacey's eyes, to her doing the ghost for two weeks without a word to me, to scheming about how to get her somewhere alone tonight so we could talk. Desperation settled on my shoulders and it was all I could do not to snatch her away from Ned and race out the door.

That we were leading double lives plagued me. It was nerve-racking. I hated what we'd been doing for the last year. Hated dating boys when I wanted to be with Stacey. Hated her and Ned being together more than she and I were. Hated the fact that this masquerade didn't stop after our senior year, but was going on still, now that we were in graduate school. The last time I'd seen Stacey alone, just after Thanksgiving, she'd talked me into being patient a little longer.

"Next semester," she'd said, "I'll have my own apartment and we can see each other whenever we want. For as long as we want. All night even."

I went along with her like I usually did, trying not to think too often about us being apart. Down the line, after we'd gotten our degrees and started living together, we wouldn't have to cover up—at least, that's the future I assumed. I'd tried to bring up the subject of us after grad school with Stacey two or three times, but somehow the conversation never took off, so we'd never really talked about it.

Lately, though, I'd been thinking about the future a lot. Never mind the meddling voice inside nagging me about the way Stacey acted that day Lynn almost caught us. Never mind the voice pointing out that Stacey couldn't even say the word *Lesbian*, couldn't fix her mouth to dignify us with the proper name, was always using the other lowdown words like *dyke, butch, bulldagger* to draw some kind of fine line, put up some kind of imaginary, protective wall. Never mind that Stacey had never really said she loved me, and had always cut me off from saying it to her. Never mind any of that. Because I had to believe that we had a future—had to believe that it wasn't crazy to think two Lesbians could have a future together. I had to believe it because...because, lately, when I thought about her, I was beginning to feel terrified of the future. Like now.

The Vandellas finished up and the dancers made their way to booths, or the bar, or stood in place waiting for the next jam to drop. James Brown had squealed the first lines of his latest hit by the time I got back to my seat. Jo's mouth was going nonstop, bending everybody's ear, but you really couldn't hear any conversation over the brass section of James Brown's band. I didn't pay attention to Jo and the rest of them for a while, that is, not until I noticed Stacey's eyes. Usually they were full of light; now, they looked flat and bottomless. I wondered about that, mulled it over until several words did manage to escape the noise and float my way: *Visit, Ned, Stacey's parents.* Now, I leaned forward hoping to catch what was being said. Only the music kept thumping and bumping, and I couldn't hear a thing.

I turned to Tweety, who was putting salt into her Schlitz and popping peanuts into her mouth. "What did Joann say?" I shouted.

Tweety put her lips close to my ear. "Ned's going to Gary for Christmas."

Ned lived in East Chicago, which was a hop, skip, and jump from Gary. Which was where Stacey lived. But so did Joann, and a zillion other folks. Even Tweety lived nearby in Hammond. Maybe, Ned was going to visit Jo and his relatives. Or, maybe, he was going to be in town partying. It wasn't unusual for somebody to throw a holiday party and have people from school showing up. Or maybe....

I stopped speculating, and asked: "Yeah, Tweety, so what?"

She shrugged, giving me that innocent, wide-eyed look that she was famous for. "I think Stacey invited him to meet her parents."

A cold blanket of dread spread itself on my heart. Stacey kept looking from Joann, to Tweety, to Ned, but was careful not to look at me. Something distant sounded in my head.

I opened my mouth to shout a question. The voice told me I didn't want to know, but I ignored it. Curiosity, after all, was my middle name, and I plunged ahead. "So, Ned," I hollered, "what's going on in Gary during Christmas?"

More than ever, he reminded me of Lassie. Any minute, I expected him to start panting. He leaned toward me, getting ready to shout out an answer when Stacey put her hand on his arm to stop him. Then, she slowly turned her eyes to me. They were deep and dark, like a drowning pool.

A few beats, and she said, clearly, her voice pitched over the music: "I've invited him."

"What for?"

You don't want to know, the voice warned me.

Smiling, Ned nudged Stacey. "Go on, you tell them."

A worm of fear uncurled at the bottom of my stomach. Stacey's eyes. They were so strange. Pulling me into their drowning pool. Maybe, it was a trick of the light; maybe, that was why they looked dark as a pit. And something was going on in her face.

"No, Ned. You say," she said so softly we all learned forward, straining to hear.

At that moment, James Brown's latest ended. Ned nodded and took a breath. "Stacey and me," he said, beaming at her, "we're engaged." He ducked his head and planted a firm kiss on her lips.

Jo whooped with glee. Tweety threw her hands up, screaming. Ned had a big, satisfied smile plastered across his face. There was no expression on Stacey's face, for a moment, and then it changed. She seemed to arrange it into a smile of sorts—one that didn't include her eyes. Eyes that held me tight. Eyes steadily pulling me under.

For a few moments, I could still hear them chattering and then I slipped inside the curve of time. Alone, inside that curve, Pain sat beside me, grinning, licking its lips in anticipation.

Later, it whispered.

I nodded, found a mask to hold my face together and tied it tightly in place.

"Congratulations," I managed to say, feeling like somebody had sucked the air out of my lungs. A tremor skipped through my body, and I steeled myself to be very still, balling my hands into fists, pushing the soles of my feet into the floor to anchor myself. I couldn't look at her.

I wouldn't. "I never guessed," I added, keeping sarcasm just barely at bay.

"Me, neither," said Jo. "When did all this happen?"

"I'll tell you later. Let's celebrate," Ned said, "Who's ready for another round?"

"Me!" squealed Tweety, clapping her hands.

"You don't have to ask me twice." Jo declared, "I'll take a rum and coke. In fact, I'll go to the bar with you. I want to hear the whole story."

"I'll have one of the same, Ned. So will Frankie," Stacey said, moving to sit beside me in Jo's chair. "I thought about telling you in the car on the way over here." The butterfly's wings lifted high as the words streamed out of Stacey's mouth in a rush. "But I decided to wait; then Ned came and wanted to announce it, so...." There was a miserable bleakness in her voice though she tried to cover it with a shiny smile.

Tweety didn't notice anything out of the ordinary, and, by this time Jo and Ned had gone off to the bar. I said nothing in response.

"When's the wedding? Tweety gushed, thrilled at the prospect.

Their voices, too loud in my ears, pushed through the air until I heard something pop. And sound stopped. Everything had stopped. Everything except Pain, who leaned toward me and stuck its razor sharp tongue inside my chest, then licked its blistered lips, savoring the taste of the wound it had made. That's when I screamed, but nobody could hear me because my throat was paralyzed. And everything had stopped.

Stopped until I found myself outside alone on the street. A few houses stood sleeping among the trees and under icy stars on a clear, black night. Except for the music trailing after me and the guffaws and shrieks of laughter drifting out of The Hole, it was quiet. I shivered, without a coat, in the frosty air. But the cold didn't matter. I needed to be out here. Needed to salve my wounds alone.

Didn't you know this would happen? The voice goaded me. Memories of that evening at The Cloister pricked at me. *Didn't you see where it would all lead?*

But I hadn't let myself think it. I'd dreamed of us growing old together.

Grief and anger and betrayal whipped me forward like a lash, pushing me along the sidewalk, pushing me to go somewhere, go nowhere, go anywhere. Agony sliced me up inside until, finally, a waterfall of tears tumbled down my face. I let them come. Covered my face and let them come.

The sound of footsteps behind me pushed my misery aside, temporarily, and I stopped crying, turning around, more than angry enough to jump down the throat of any would-be night bandit. But it was no bandit. At least, not that kind that takes your money. It was Stacey coming toward me, head bowed so I couldn't see her face, coatless shoulders hunched, and arms crossed against her chest to ward off the cold.

When she was within three or four steps of me, she stopped, without looking up, standing back a ways from me. I didn't think the distance was for the sake of appearance. Maybe she was afraid I'd haul off and hit her or something. In a way, I wanted to, yet I couldn't and I really wasn't up to that kind of drama. So, the both of us stood under the street light, hiding behind silence, waiting to see what the other would do or say. It took her a long time to look up at me, and when she raised her head at last, I saw something harsh and ruinous in her face.

"Don't hate me," she said softly, her green eyes looking like a brewing summer storm. "Please."

I didn't know what I was going to say until the words came: "Why didn't you tell me? Why like this, in front of all those people?" I hated lying. It made me crazy. And she'd done that. Lied by omission.

The mole on her eyebrow lifted and she shrugged. "I didn't plan it this way. I didn't know he was going to be here, let alone want to announce it tonight." She grimaced, and put the tips of her fingers to her head like somebody puzzling out the answer to a complex equation. "I wanted to tell you. A dozen times in the past few weeks. I just couldn't find a way." She stopped looking at me, glanced at the ground for a moment, and then shook her head again. "And...I guess. Well, I guess, really, I was scared to tell you."

"What were you scared of?"

Weariness weaved in and out of her words, as if she'd had a long, hard battle. "Of you. And of us. I know you, Frankie. You'd have tried to talk me out of getting engaged. And..." Something in her face worked mightily to force the words out of her mouth. "and I might have let you." I heard the fear in her voice. And, saw it again in her eyes.

Might have let me? What was she saying? She came close to me, lifted the fingers of my hand and touched them to her lips. The gesture startled me, startled me in its boldness, startled me in its obvious affection. It was a gesture she'd only done sometimes. And only in private. The Stacey I knew would never risk exposure by doing it in public. Someone could have seen us. Why was she doing it now? Did she love me after all? Maybe, there was still a chance. My head suddenly ached with confusion.

"Stacey just don't do it!" I blurted out. Silently, I had begun a supplication, a prayer—a bargaining with the gods. I would make a sacrifice, any sacrifice, to keep us together. "Don't marry him. We can be together. You don't have to be with him!" Tears stood in my eyes again.

She dropped my hand and smiled sadly. "Yes, I do. I have to be with him."

She sounded so sure. As if somebody had passed a sentence on her. "Are you pregnant?"

She threw her head back and laughed. It was a bitter sound. And full of despair. "I haven't even slept with him. Haven't been able to bring myself to do it."

"Then why?" My question sounded like a desperate plea—a cry in the wilderness. And it was.

When she touched her hand to my cheek, I had my answer. Because I saw the shadow of cold fear change her eyes in a heart-sinking way. I knew I had lost her before she said it. "You know the reason." Her voice was ragged, a thing torn and shredded. "Because I can't keep thinking about you. I can't! It's too *painful*. And—and so I *had* to do something to end it. Because, because you won't."

So that invisible thing inside had beaten her in the end. Made her give us up. With despair and grief surging up into my throat, I wanted to turn my face up to the night and howl. I wanted to shriek, bellow, scream, curse the gods. No, not the gods. The world. Curse what it had done to Stacey's insides. And what it made her do to us.

"Come back inside," she said, her hand on my shoulder. "You can't stay out here."

Raging anger clawed its way up from my belly and I shook her hand away from me. "What do you care?" I spit out at her.

I saw the pain washing over her face in waves. And though I hadn't planned it, I knew a second of bittersweet triumph because I had hurt her. But its taste turned my stomach. Still, the burning rainstorm inside me drove me to strike at her again.

"Get away from me!" I screamed. "Go back to your—your fiancé!" My voice shattered on the word and something broke inside me.

I looked into her green eyes once more. Those mesmerizing eyes that had always pulled me to her. I looked into them for some sign that she would change her mind. That there was still hope. But I only saw bewilderment there. Finally, I turned my back on her, a river of tears on my face.

Stacey hesitated, for a moment, and walked away.

It came to me then that nothing would ever be the same. That we wouldn't, as I had dreamed, grow old together. Realizing that made me tremble, suddenly, for I had no idea how I would navigate this new place where Stacey would not be. I was afraid then. Afraid of loneliness. Afraid of the path ahead. I looked up. The stars blazed like crystal fire against the black of night. In the stillness, I could hear Stacey's footsteps receding.

And her going away crackled in my ears like distant thunder.

Fried Buzzard Nights

Sometimes, now, on boiling nights when the hot Santa Ana winds come swooping down on Los Angeles from the desert, I remember being at Allen's Sycamore Tavern in the relentless, humid heat of Indiana. Those were fried buzzard nights. When Allen's overworked air-conditioning simply gave up and refused to wheeze out another drop of cool breath; when I sat laughing, smoking, and drinking scotch on the rocks; when sweat soaked my underarms, while rivulets of it ran down between my breasts.

In Evansville, my favorite hangout was Allen's. I can see it, still: A tiny, red-shingled bar with a worn-around-the-edges look to it, hunched up on the corner of Denby and Sycamore streets in the middle of a bleak landscape. Squatting on either side of the tavern, houses—little square boxes or shotgun rectangles—leaned plaintively against each other like shell-shocked survivors. Inches away from their porches and from doorways that grimly kept their own counsel, you could see stunning medleys of flowers—mouth watering red roses, huge clusters of periwinkle snowballs, rainbows of gladiolas—so beautiful they mocked their stark, unlovely surroundings. Across the street from the bar there was a tiny, forlorn playground, equipped with a stringless basketball hoop, rusting swings, and a picnic table groaning under the combined weight of constant exposure to the elements, and the continuous neglect of the city's recreation department. Next to the playground stood a barbecue stand with the approximate dimensions of an outhouse, abandoned by a dozen or so previous entrepreneurs who couldn't pay their dues to The Man. They were gone, but they'd left the peeling, tin sign.

Inside the tavern, the layout was pocket-sized cozy. To the left of the entrance, there was a bar long enough for six stools. In the whole place, you'd find maybe a dozen tables and a jukebox. A tiny kitchen was back of the bar where Bea turned out baskets of crunchy, golden-fried chicken, platters of cornmeal-crusted, fried catfish, and mounds of creamy-smooth potato salad. With just enough mustard, pickle and celery to satisfy my soul. Every now and then, on weekday afternoons, when only a few of us were there, somebody who'd gone hunting might bring in a barbecued possum or roasted coon, having soaked the forest critter in vinegar and water long enough to take the toughness out of the meat, while leaving in its "wild" taste. Then, there'd be a shared feast with stories all around. I didn't like the wild-tasting meat. but I did like the bar. It was Black, working class, and Midwestern with a distinct, small town, neighborhood flavor to it. Not outright countrified though.

People wondered why I went there, I suppose. Why I went was simple enough. I went looking for the other half of my Blackness. The part that I sensed was the core of me. The root. The center I needed to find my balance. To make me whole. I went there looking for the people that I knew would be there. The ones Mama had encrypted with secrecy, with tantalizing mystery, by the tightness around her eyes and mouth. The ones Daddy had slipped out to party with at night. The ones you wouldn't see at Sunday church or fraternity balls. The blues-making women. The back alley, dice-throwing men. The good-time folk who gave the devil a run for his money.

But there was something else there, I remember. Something that found me: Alcohol. Waiting to take me. Enclose me. Ensnare me forever, if it could.

At night, sometimes, when the Santa Ana winds caress me with smoldering breath, I close my eyes and I am there again with Clyde Dixon, dressed in hospital whites, perched like a pelican at the end of the bar, waiting for his daily deliverance, a tall glass of Johnnie Walker Red and water. There again with Sylvester Smallings, mustached, brown lips turned up into a Sylvester the Cat grin, chugging down a shot glass of Old Forester, then carefully turning the glass mouth-down on the bar. There again, watching the owner, Anderson Allen, midnight-skinned, bespeckled, tall as an ostrich, leaning on the bar, gossiping with one of the customers. There again, watching the bartenders, Les and Jay, pouring liquor that cascades like a waterfall as it splashes into glasses of cracked ice. I am there watching the wino they called Cheese, darting in as silent as a shadow, to get a quick glass of Mad Dog 20-20, then slipping out like the ghost he'd soon become.

Sometimes, in August heat, memory works juju in my night dreams; conjures times gone by, places of old, and ghosts beloved. Sometimes, dream memory works its night magic and takes me back there. Back there, where you can hear our laughter still rumbling, roaring, rolling through the room. Back there, where our laughter still lives. In my dreams.

Scotch on the Rocks

1. Night Flyer

I was late for the play at Evansville College, my dashboard clock told me. I muttered a curse. If I hadn't had that last drink at Allen's tonight, I wouldn't be crunching the accelerator to gain some extra minutes driving down Lincoln Avenue. The rain-spattered windshield had me squinting to keep inside the road's yellow line. I blinked to clear my vision, easing up on the accelerator pedal a bit. It was annoying that the damn line kept wiggling. How was I supposed to drive on the right side if it didn't stay straight? The frantic swish-swish of the wipers dancing across the windshield was getting on my nerves. If only I could switch on some music. That would drown them out. But the radio was on the blink. To calm myself down, I stuck a Pell Mell between my lips, pushed in the cigarette lighter, and waited. In a few seconds, it popped out and I lowered my eyes to grope for it. My fingers found the lighter and as I looked up at the road again, out of the darkness, a parked Volkswagen materialized inches away on my right. Startled, I jerked hard on the steering wheel just in time to keep from side-swiping the car. A shaky breath escaped my lips as I gripped the wheel firmly with both hands.

"That was a narrow escape," I whispered to myself.

The light turned red ahead at Kentucky Avenue and Lincoln; I braked and tossed the cigarette in the ashtray.

134

The urge to smoke had evaporated. A peep at the clock, while I waited for the light to change, needled me, once more, to keep hurrying. It was in my favor that the streets folded up this time of night in Evansville. No cars out and about meant I could go faster for the rest of the way down Lincoln. I gazed at the red light. *Come on, come on. How long are you gonna stay red?* Ahead, streetlights threw out yellow shafts of light. A couple of cars sped across the intersection in front of me, their tires whistling on black pavement that glistened with raindrops. My eyes shifted to the painted line ahead down the middle of the street. It still shimmied like a snake, so I closed one eye and looked again. The line seemed to straighten.

"No more shimmy, shimmy like my sister Kate," I bragged to the empty car.

The light turned yellow. Then green. My toes pushed down on the accelerator and the car jumped forward to cross Kentucky Avenue, the line of demarcation between Black folks' home ground and White folks' territory. Outside my windshield, I noticed the outlined shapes of trees streaking by, then melting into pools of black shadows. Further back, big, brightly lit houses sat comfortably on broad expanses of lawn. It was getting hard for me to make out what was shadow and what was substance. I scooted forward, squinting. Because the rain was now no more than a few drops, my car's wipers began to screech and scrape. I twisted the control dial to intermittent and glanced at the clock. It was five minutes after eight and the play would be starting now. The speedometer needle pointed at thirty-nine miles per hour. There'd be no more stoplights for a few blocks, so I could get away with just a little bit more speed. *Must go faster,* I told myself and pressed down on the accelerator.

Then, out of the corner of my eye, I thought I saw a puppy dart out into the street. I slammed my foot on the brake, hard. And as soon as I did, the car skidded to the right. For a moment, my mind froze. Was I supposed to turn the car into the skid or away from it? I couldn't remember. Following instinct, I steered left instead of right. The Pinto spun like a whirligig, weaving across the street's middle line. Everything was out of control. Not far ahead, I saw the lights of an oncoming car. Desperate to get out of harm's way, I hit the accelerator, at the same time, tugging at the wheel. A corner appeared out of the darkness and I jerked right sharply, swerving in. *Too fast!* My mind screamed as the car barreled toward parked cars on my right. To compensate, I pulled the wheel to the left, but too far. The car surged into a driveway and up the incline of a yard. Wind rushed past my cheeks from the half-opened windows. Suddenly, a huge magnolia tree loomed up out of the yard, directly in my car's path. I tried pulling the steering wheel to the right to avoid the tree, but it wasn't quite enough. Bark flew and I closed my eyes, hearing the sound of screaming metal as the Pinto plowed in and sideswiped the magnolia. I could feel the driver's door buckling while shattered glass popped like firecrackers; shards flew into my hair, fell on my coat, and into my lap. The car came to rest with the driver's door jammed shut, and its nose bulldozed into the magnolia. I groaned when I realized the car and I were sitting in the front yard of a Georgian style, two-story mansion. *Shit-a-mile!* No way could I play this off; these folks would be calling the cops for sure. Maybe they wouldn't smell the liquor though. I fumbled for some breath mints as a young, blonde woman came running out of the front door to find out if I needed an ambulance. I told her I didn't, then threw a couple of mints in my mouth as I climbed out on the passenger side. It was gonna be a long night.

2. Q. and A.

A young man with sallow skin sat before me, staring down at a pamphlet. I inspected him warily. Sunbeams streaming through the window bounced off his straight, jet-black hair. The November afternoon sun backlit the man the way a Hollywood cameraman might, sculpting his face in granite planes and hollows. Although he wore the uniform of an older, corporation man—a gray suit with narrow lapels, a crisp, white shirt and a tightly-knotted, navy tie—he looked to be about my age, in his late twenties, but a bit frayed around the edges. I looked around me. The office was a cubbyhole: A desk, a couple of chairs, a tall, gray file cabinet in the corner, and an overflowing wastebasket. The office was tiny enough for my I-hate-cramped-places phobia to kick into gear, but it was checked by the huge window behind his desk. Without shade or blinds for cover, it opened wide on the levee and the Ohio River beyond to give you the illusion of space.

The air hummed with silence. It felt surreal, like I'd been plopped down in the middle of a movie set where the director had called for quiet. Pinpricks of painful humiliation stabbed me every time I thought about the driving under the influence ticket that had got me here. I drummed my fingers on the big, red purse in my lap, wishing I could comfort myself with a cigarette. But, a few minutes ago, when I'd pulled out my Pell Mells, the man had said right off that I couldn't: "It's against the rules. This is a smoke-free office," he'd said, his eyes looking like a bottomless, black pool.

What a bitch! Sentenced to a session with an alcohol counselor in a smoke-free office! Who thought up this kind of torture anyway? My toes twitched anxiously. I glared at him. What was he reading anyhow? Did it have something to do with the questions he'd said he'd be asking me? I crossed my legs because I didn't know what to do with myself. God, I wanted this over quick, so I could head out for Allen's. Today was Friday and the eagle was flying; people would be swooping in on its wings, ready to trade those dollar bills for a good time. Besides that, a scotch on the rocks would soothe my jumpy nerves just fine about now.

Without preamble, the counselor spoke into the silence. "When you drink, how many would you say you ordinarily might have?"

I swallowed and laced my fingers together to hide my shaking hands. "Two. Maybe, three." The lie rolled off my tongue as easy as pie.

For a few beats, the black light in his eyes searched my face. That steady gaze set my toes to itching. I rubbed the front of my right foot up and down the back of my left leg, hoping for relief. At the window, blue-bellied clouds had drifted into view. While I watched them, he wrote something down.

Looking down at an open file folder on the desk, he began again. "You crashed into a tree the night of the accident." The man paused, looked up at me, and asked: "How many drinks did you have that night?"

The question embarrassed me. I mumbled an answer, then began to inspect the new red boots I had on for scuff marks.

He didn't let me get away with it. "How many?"

I lifted my head. "Four, I believe." Actually, I knew I'd had more like six or seven drinks that night. Desperate to escape his bottomless, black eyes, I shifted mine back to the window. The large, single pane was almost invisible, as if you could dive right out of it and into the river's rippling, dove-gray waves.

After flipping to another page in the file folder, he said, "This is your second D.U.I. Are you sure about that?"

Hot anger bubbled up under my skin. I played it off by shrugging and smoothing my skirt. What the hell was this jive turkey tryin to say? I didn't want to hit the puppy that's why I had the accident!

The counselor studied the pamphlet on his desk again. When he looked at me this time, his expression was questioning. "Why did you have four that night when ordinarily you drink less? Was something bothering you?"

"Nothing was wrong," I said, hoping I wouldn't get caught in the lies I was weaving. Sweat popped out under my armpits as my eyes slid away from his to the window. I pictured myself leaping out of it into the Ohio River, then swimming away with easy, deliberate strokes.

He shifted in his seat and smoothed his tie a bit. In an off-handed tone, he threw out another question, "How long have you been drinking?"

Twelve years of my past flared up and a tide of liquor swept by: Chugalugging rum with Steve before a dance, sipping Seagram's Seven undercover in Carol's dorm room, guzzling vodka with Shari at a house party. Half-pints, fifths, and quarts of whiskey, rum, gin, scotch. Cans of Schlitz, Colt 45, Budweiser, Champale. Sipping martinis, gimlets, daiquiris, champagne. Drinking at the bar after work, in the kitchen playing Bid Whist, outside at the softball games on Sundays, in the living room on Saturday afternoons. Cocktails, nightcaps, toddies, and hair of the dog that bit you all washed by in waves. An ocean of memories. A smile almost touched my lips at the thought of them, but other, more recent things flowed in around the edges, spoiling memories of the good times: Hangovers, memory lapses, car accidents, the shakes, guilt driving me to say I'd only have one drink and then waking the next day to realize that one had somehow turned into ten or twelve. I wrinkled my nose at the rotten smell of my own shame. *What happened?* I asked myself silently. *It used to be so much fun.*

The man leaned forward, pressing me for an answer: "How long? Months? Years?"

I wished he would stop being nosey, stop poking around into my business. "A few years," I said, avoiding his question with vagueness. How long was I gonna have to sit through these stupid-ass questions?

He consulted the pamphlet and came at me again. "When did you take your first drink?"

I stared at him, realizing that I wasn't going to be able to think fast enough to get him off me. The questions, the probing jabbed my insides like a knife. I could feel a sharp ache in my side, draining away my resolve to sidestep him.

"Do you remember?"

It didn't matter if I told him the truth this time. "Twelve years ago. At college." Hearing it was eerie somehow. *Was it that long ago?*

"First drink at college." He repeated, making a note.

"When I was a freshman. Before a fraternity dance," I added. And reminded myself: *In the cab with Steve.* He'd asked me if I knew how to drink and I'd said yes. Then he'd poured a paper cup full of Bacardi's rum, splashed some coke in it, and smiled, nodding for me to try it. The rum had burned my tongue.

"What kind of experience was it for you, good or bad?" The counselor asked.

"Good," I said, but it really wasn't. The moment Steve had said, "Drink up," I'd felt scared. Like I'd signed up for a big contest that I didn't know how to win. Scared because I was an imposter, posing as a sophisticated lady all dressed up in a rose, satin cocktail dress with long, black gloves. Scared shitless, looking down at the dark liquid in the cup because I was a liar. I'd never had a drink before. But I drank it all up like he told me to, and ended up with my head hanging over the toilet stool, my stomach heaving, trying to vomit the stuff up.

Remembering brought back smothering feelings of shame. To push them away, I let my eyes wander to my escape hatch—the office window. More clouds had linked up with the blue-bellies. The new gray-colored ones had fat, dark bottoms. I wondered if it was going to rain and if I had an umbrella in the car.

"Do you mostly drink alone, or with others—say at dinner, at a bar, something like that?"

His question pulled me back into the room. I uncrossed and re-crossed my legs to give myself time to consider whether to lie or not. "Sometimes alone, other times at bars or at dinner with other people."

Without pause, he launched into the next one. "How often do you drink? Every day? A couple of times a week?"

I blinked at his attack. It took a moment before I could put together an answer. "Once or twice a week." The lie came out of me in a squeaky, uneven voice.

He gave me a doubtful look. "Once or twice? You don't drink more than that typically in a week?"

"No," I said sealing the lie with defiance and a good deal of resentment.

A distant sadness glistened in his eyes. Then, his face became even more grave and still. "Do you think you have a drinking problem?"

White heat exploded in my chest. To keep my hands from going for his neck, I choked my purse for dear life and bit my tongue. Mr. Langley, my boss and the Director of the Library, thought I had a drinking problem. He'd told me so as big as you please. Called me into his office two weeks ago after the accident to let me know his secretary, Miss Hardy, had seen my name in the paper under the court records. I could still picture the two of them tsk-tsk-tsking about my name in the paper. *Shit-a-mile! What kind of secretary combs the local rag for gossip to report it back to her boss anyway?* I was still seething with resentment. I had to concede he had a right to call me on the carpet. It did look bad to have your Community Relations Coordinator going to court for drunk driving. All the same, when that little Napoleon had fixed me with a severe look that made me feel lower than dirt, I'd felt like slapping his ass into next week.

The counselor repeated his question: "Do you think you have a drinking problem?"

I didn't know what to say. Anger and shame fought it out in my head while a red-hot poker burned in my chest.

"Please answer the—"

"No, I don't," I almost shouted. Then, I took a breath and stammered out the rest. "At least, I, I don't think so." *Where had that come from?*

He closed the folder and lifted his eyes to mine. "Would you like to quit?"

Quit? My mind nudged the idea like it was an alien thing, and white-hot fear gushed up, like lava, surging into every cell of my body. *Quit?* Scotch was my Linus blanket. My protector. My mind zoomed away, imagining a life, a future without scotch. A future that looked like a long, dark, winding tunnel. One that was unknowable and unpredictable. Who knew what might be waiting? Most likely, scary things you couldn't see coming. *Quit scotch?* My mind scrambled away from the idea as if it was a fully-hooded, swaying cobra poised in my path. I just couldn't feature it. How the hell did anybody just up and quit?

Aloud, I said, "Uh, uh. I don't think so. Why should I give up partying? Everybody wants to have a good time. Right?"

He stared at me as if he were contemplating something; then he licked his lips and said, "Sure, people want to have a good time, but alcoholism is a serious disease. Deadly, in fact. I think you ought to take a hard look at your drinking."

I wanted to cuss his raggedy-white-ass out, calling me an alcoholic right to my face. But I didn't want a bad report to go to the judge, so I said, in my meekest voice, "You're right, sir."

He shuffled some papers on his desk and put them into a neat stack, then, looked at me once more, as if he were taking my measure. "Okay, Miss Lennon. You can go." He swiveled his chair around to the file cabinet in a gesture of dismissal.

Glancing at my watch, I rose quickly from the chair. It was a relief to see that I'd be able to catch the five o'clock crowd at Allen's. Before I turned to go, my eyes were drawn to the window once more. The late afternoon sun had stained the sky with oranges and reds.

2. What's Goin On?

The five o'clock crew at Allen's Lounge was off and running. The place buzzed like a busy hive. Compared to the worn and threadbare Sycamore Tavern, this new bar of Allen's was almost classy-looking. It was larger and brighter, a far cry from the old tavern hunched on the corner like a dark, ancient crone. Despite the "Lounge" that Allen had adopted to signal a higher status for his bar, those who considered themselves high-class snubbed Allen's in favor of Club Paradise on Lincoln. Basically, the crowd at Allen's remained the same: Blue collar with a smattering of white collar here and there.

What's goin on? I heard Marvin Gaye ask over the chattering hum of the crowd. *Home free! That's what's goin on,* I answered in my head while situating myself on a barstool. *No alcohol counselor and his stupid questions around here!* I nodded hello to the regulars lining the bar like pigeons waiting for bread crusts. Behind the bar, Allen, tall as an ostrich and dark as bitter chocolate, counted bills and change to balance the cash register. Jay iced down the beer while Les, looking like a sad-eyed, basset hound, poured up half-dozen drink orders as Katie, the waitress, reeled them off.

I lit a cigarette and glanced up at the huge, lighted mirror in front of me; the crowd's doings immediately snagged my attention. Scattered at tables, men in blue or gray work uniforms, just getting off from work at Whirlpool or Alcoa, drank quarts of Budweiser or shots of whiskey, smoked cigarettes, traded lies, hawked the women, and speculated on which one might want a just-for-tonight lover. The women, in bright colors, sat in groups of two's and three's, cutting their eyes at each other, whispering behind their hands, or throwing their heads back in noisy laughter. Most of them sipped pretty drinks—the kind I never had much use for—like Tom Collins or Tequila Sunrise, although some toyed with a glass of beer.

I caught Jay's eye and winked. He was a beauty. An x-rated honey-dripper. Cinnamon skin, thick eyelashes, naturally arched eyebrows, sculpted, full lips. And so good in bed that I could pretend my woman-jones didn't exist. Sometimes, all his sexiness and beauty triggered my inferiority complexes. At other times, my ego swelled with the idea that a sugah-lump like him had picked me to be his woman.

"What's up?" I asked as he came toward me

He shrugged, slapping a napkin on the counter. "Gonna be jumpin in here tonight. Allen's got me working the night shift, so I won't get by your place until 2:30. You want your usual? It's on me."

"Yeah, scotch on the—"

He finished it. "Rocks, lemon slice, water back."

"What else?" I smiled.

He grinned at me and started to pour. As he did, a voice hollered out.

"Give her another!" It was Sylvester sitting at the other end of the bar; he slammed two quarters down for Jay. I waved at Syl and nodded my thanks. He, in turn, lifted his shot glass ceremoniously in salute.

Jay put another glass down beside the first. Watching him pour a drink was mesmerizing. He made it high art. With a magician's flourish, he tossed the scotch bottle from one hand to the other, lifted it high in the air, and flicked his wrist to let the liquor flow in an even stream, first into one glass, then, without missing a beat, into the other. I'd seen him do it a thousand times and he'd never spilled a drop.

Jay put two drinks in front of me, went down the bar to collect for it, rang up the order, and trotted off to the john. I gestured for Syl to come over and take the empty seat beside me. He stood and hitched up his pants the way he always did, then, strolled over.

When he reached me, he said: "Gotta go. Got business to take care of."

"What? On a Friday night?" I was disappointed that he was leaving. Syl was one of my favorite drinking buddies

He shrugged. "Catch you later, sis."

On his way out, he stopped at a table to slap the backs of some men. I shifted my sight from Syl's retreat to the mirror behind the bar. It ran the length of the wall. The bottles, in front of it, artfully arranged in stair-step fashion, caught my eye. Like ladies of the night displaying their wares to the highest bidder, the shimmering liquor winked and promised good times: Scotch in emerald green bottles, whiskey in topaz brown bottles, vodka and gin in diamond-clear bottles. I picked up my glass and sipped.

Nothing like the first scotch of the day, I told myself while savoring the bitter, slightly oily taste of J & B.

A good feeling began to settle over me. But before the good feeling could make itself at home, out of nowhere, I heard the counselor ask: *Do you want to quit?*

Spooked, I glanced over my shoulder, frowning as I scanned the crowd. Was that asshole of an alcohol counselor in here? Did he follow me to Allen's? But, no. There were only Black folks here, getting down to some serious partying. I stared into the golden liquid in my glass. *Do you want to quit?* He'd asked me. An icy tremor passed through me. How could I give it up? My palms felt clammy and I wiped them together.

There'd been times when I'd thought about it. Especially when I'd come into Allen's, and somebody at the bar would ask me if I remembered what I'd done the night before. I hated that question. It shamed me. They knew what I'd done, but I didn't. It was unnerving because a big, black hood had dropped down over my brain. What I'd done the night before was gone. Wiped clean. When someone asked me, I'd drop my eyes, afraid that I'd made a fool of myself. Afraid that somebody was going to rib me for it and I wouldn't be able to, couldn't play it off. How could I when last night was a bunch of empty pages scrolling in my head?

I pulled on my cigarette. Why couldn't I remember? What was happening? Maybe I should seriously consider quitting. But when that line of thought came to mind, I had to have a drink since thinking about quitting was unnerving. By the time I'd finished drinking and thinking, mother scotch had moved the whole idea to the back burner.

What's goin on? Marvin asked me, his voice fading on the last notes of the song. I took a long swallow of scotch, almost draining the glass as The Isley's kicked "Love the

One You With" into high gear. It was then that the door swung open so hard that the hinges squeaked and sang. I turned my head to see who was coming in. There at the entrance stood Jay's wife—a harmless-looking, brown terrier with the soul of a war dog. For a millisecond, she was motionless; then, she swooped in.

Thank God, Jay was in the john. If she had come in a few minutes earlier, she'd have caught me sitting here carrying on with him. But she didn't need to catch me to know I was guilty. When Jay was here, nine times out of ten, I was, too. Marsha knew, like everybody else in Evansville, that I was Jay's sideline woman. It was a common practice. Husbands took lovers; wives looked the other way. Marsha didn't frequent the bars, so ordinarily Allen's Lounge was safe territory for me and Jay. But not, it seemed, today. In the mirror, I watched her double-timing it straight to me, her jaws tighter than Dick's hatband. She stomped up beside me and stopped, hand on her hip, glaring. Without looking at her, I lifted my glass to drink, weighing the threat of danger her presence signaled while cold sweat inched down my stomach.

"What the hell," she addressed me in ringing tones, loud enough for everyone to take notice, "do you think you're doin in here with Jay?"

At the sound of her voice, the bar's noisy crowd suddenly came to attention, slipping into the I-was-a-witness mode, drinks forgotten as eyes turned to watch local drama.

Marsha moved a step closer. "Ain't I tole you bout this shit before?"

Survival instinct screamed for me to get the hell out of the bar, but my feet had turned to concrete. Careful not to look her in the face, I took a drag on my Pell Mell and tapped some ashes off the tip.

She took the drama up a notch, playing to every person in the room. "I hope," she proclaimed, "you don't think I'ma jus sit back in some corner while you fuck around with my husband."

I could feel her breath on my neck. Was she going to jump me? My heart was thumping in time with the record's beat. Since I'd never been a fighter, I had zero confidence about myself when it came to fisty-cuffs, but if she made a move to beat my ass, would I just sit here and let her?

The crowd hung with bated breath on every word. She huffed and puffed for them. "I'ma tell you one more time to leave Jay alone."

I kept silent, gambling that she'd interpret my silence as browbeaten humiliation and leave me be.

She pronounced her final threat with a flourish. "Don't let me have to tell you bout this shit no more!" A dramatic pause, and then: "You hear me?"

The challenge hung in the air. Despite the fact that I was shivering in my boots, the smart-ass in me finally reared its head, ready to deliver me to the hangman's noose. I opened my mouth with the intention of sarcastically assuring Marsha that I had, indeed, heard her. But Jay glided up before I could say a word, and quickly steered her out of the bar.

The door slammed behind them, and the crowd came back to life, jabbering excitedly. Although I felt frazzled, the mirror showed me looking cool as a cucumber: Permed hair pulled back into a long pony tail, Cleopatra eye makeup unsmeared, gold earrings dangling. Underneath it all, fright churned my guts like a washing machine. To steady my galloping heartbeat, I finished off the rest of the scotch in glass number one, pushed it away, and pulled glass number two into drinking position.

Katie, on her way to put in order, stopped beside me. "Don't let Marsha bother you. She be all bark and no bite."

"You think so?" I asked, glad she was rallying round me. It softened the hard edge of guilt that poked my ribs when I thought about Jay's wife and family.

"Hell, yeah," she said, looking for all the world like somebody's teddy bear as she waddled toward the waitress station. "Don't sweat the small stuff, baby girl!"

On the jukebox, The Isley's played out and Gladys Knight swung in on the grapevine with the Pips backing her up. I took a big sip out of scotch number two, feeling a nice buzz as I watched the boogying on the dance floor. Before long, Jay rushed in and trotted behind the bar, giving Allen an apologetic look. Allen shook his head in disgust while Jay began to busy himself with glasses that needed washing, and beer that needed icing.

I blew out a long stream of cigarette smoke. Wisps glided together. A pale face with deep, black, mocking eyes materialized and floated just above my drink. It looked like the alcohol counselor. I stared, fearfully, at the apparition.

Do you think drinking will make The Corners go away? It asked.

Why was I was seeing things? And how did it know about The Corners? Nobody knew about The Corners. *Go away!* I shouted wordlessly, shutting my eyes. I didn't like to think about The Corners. Although Marsha had rattled my cage, she wasn't the scariest thing in my life. The Corners were. I was twenty-nine years old, and scared to death of the lightless places where I'd shoved things in my life that I couldn't deal with; scared of The Corners— shadowy, murky places, where I'd hidden the truth about me. The memory of Stacey languished there. Dreams and desires lay abandoned there. Unclaimed and suffocating, my life lay buried there, gasping and clawing to break free. Pitch-black, dark and deep, The Corners haunted me. I was afraid of them and the things dying there. When I opened my eyes, and looked at the apparition, it grimaced at me with disapproval.

Why are you living your life in a bar? It asked.

I'm not! I screamed at it silently, and the face broke apart, leaving tendrils of smoke drifting in the air. Thoroughly shaken, I gulped down most of my drink.

Charlie, standing nearby, stumbled over. He studied my face. "You look like you could use another," he said to me, swaying on unsteady legs.

"Yeah, guess I could," I agreed. I needed it to calm the dread trickling, like acid, into my stomach. Besides, I never refused a freebie.

"Les," Charlie said, "set her up. I'm buyin. And bring me another rum and coke."

As Les filled the order, the head of the alcohol counselor suddenly popped out of thin air. The disembodied head reminded me of the Cheshire cat in *Alice in Wonderland*. I blinked at the hallucination.

How much do you drink? It demanded to know, black eyes fixed on the almost-empty scotch glass in front of me.

Charlie yammered away, apparently noticing nothing out of the ordinary. I took a deep breath, grabbed the drink in front of me, and chugalugged it, hoping the head of the counselor would vanish.

It didn't. Instead, it continued interrogating me. *How much do you drink?* It pressed, dark eyes flashing, daring me to lie.

Not as much as Charlie. He's a stone drunk! I shot back in my defense. I always marveled that it took so little for Charlie to get high; after two or so, he'd be three sheets in the wind, where it would usually take half-dozen or more for me to get there. The head scowled at the thread of my

150

argument. I ignored the scowl and taunted: *Well, Mr. Alcohol Counselor, what'll you say to Charlie? Tell him he has a serious disease? Ask him if he wants to give it up?*

Les put fresh drinks in front of Charlie and me.

How many drinks does that make for you? The head asked quietly while its eyes probed my insides like a scalpel.

Just leave me alone, I snarled, my stomach trembling like jello.

The thing stared at me, its face fixed in a grim, schoolmarm expression. I felt like it was dumping a load of squirming guilt into my stomach. God! I wished I'd stop seeing things. It was ruining everything.

Charlie pushed a dollar bill to Les and picked up his rum and coke. "Be seein ya," he said to me. "I'm playin pool over there with Marcellus."

"Okay.Thanks, Charlie," I said.

Allen's door opened, and I turned away from the floating head to see Billy strolling in. I waved at him, then looked back at the spot where the counselor's head had been hovering. But it had disappeared. I sighed, deeply relieved.

Billy sat on one of the empty barstools nearest the door and ordered a coke. I checked out his appearance. You'd never guess by the way he was dressed that he operated and owned an automobile repair shop. If your car had a dent, or a bent fender, he was your man. Accidents seemed to hover around me—the magnolia tree accident being a case in point, so Billie had made a good piece of change off me. Everybody knew that there were side benefits in taking your car to his place. For one, he made the best barbecue in town, bar none. Not only did you get his barbeque when you took your car to him, you'd also get to share his bottle or, if you preferred, the beer in the fridge. I passed on his beer, but never on his bottle. Now, Billy was definitely somebody who drank more than I did.

Though it didn't seem to get in the way of his work because when he did my cars, you couldn't tell that I'd misjudged here and there, and sideswiped a car, a tree, or run into a house.

Lately, though, there was a change in Billy's drinking habits. Used to be, he'd order a double Four Roses and coke. Not now though. He'd told me he'd stopped. And his appearance showed it. The old Billy always came to the bar in his wrinkled coveralls, stained with engine oil and paint dust; the new Billy showed up, pressed and righteously put together, in a suit and shined shoes. Like today.

Something tugged at me to get up and go over to him. Without consciously thinking about it, I moved to his side just as Les shoved a glass of coke at him.

"What's up, Billy?" I greeted him. It was always good to see Billy. Something about him reminded me of Uncle Matt. Maybe it was his maple-colored skin.

Smiling hugely, he said, "Nothing much. I'm lookin for one of my customers. Ain't you off early? Thought they didn't let you outta that library until six."

Since he'd fixed my car himself, Billy knew I had to go to court. "The judge sent me to some alcohol counselor, so I had to take off."

I watched him drain some of the coke Les had put in front of him. Billy puzzled me; he didn't act like he missed the ole Roses at all. An icy finger touched the back of my neck and I shivered, wondering: *Was it that easy for him just to stop cold?*

A couple of guys near the pool table suddenly laughed loudly. I jumped at the sound, and I thought I saw Billy give me, for a second, a strange glance.

"There's my customer, Marcellus," he said. "We got business." He glanced at my empty hands. I'd left my drinks at my seat. "Want a drink?"

"Sure. I never turn down a drink," I said automatically.

Billy caught Les's eye and nodded at me. Les set a whiskey glass on the bar, shoveled in some ice and poured my J & B in it. After Les put the drink in front of me, Billy pulled out change, dropped it on the bar, and heaved himself up.

As he started walking away, the alcohol counselor's face floated up into my vision. I saw his pale, stern mouth. *I think*, the mouth said, *that you ought to take a look at your drinking.*

The words made me quiver inside, like an arrow striking true to its mark. Before I knew what I was doing, I was on my feet, and at Billy's heels. "Billy," I said, gesturing for him to move a discreet distance away from any listening ears.

"Yeah?"

"I wanna ask you something."

He waited.

I lowered my voice. "Was it hard?"

He looked confused. "What?"

I felt a knot growing in my chest. "Quitting," I whispered, my throat constricting. "Quitting the drinking."

He gave me a sharp look. "Why you wanna know?"

I shrugged, icicles in my stomach. I couldn't have told him why; I didn't even know I was going to ask, but I needed an answer.

"Was it?" I pressed him.

Instead of answering me, Billy stood, as if he were rooted to the spot, hands in his pockets, staring at the floor. Some indefinable thing, dark as batwings blotting out the moon, flew across his face and twisted it, for a moment, into a mask of pain. At the sight of his reaction, I winced, dread touching my heart. *Maybe it would be better*, I thought, *if I didn't know. Maybe I should tell Billy never mind*. But looking at Billy I didn't think I could call the question back now. Katie passed close by, threw us both a strange look, and kept walking.

"Yeah," Billy finally said, on a breath that was hoarse and strangling. "It was hard."

My chest rippled in fear at his words. At what was behind them. At the things he wasn't saying. Once more, Billy turned to leave. But there was more I needed to ask though I didn't know exactly what. So I couldn't let him leave. If he went, the knot of terror swelling in my chest would burst.

"Billy," I put my hand on his arm to stop him, and the words tumbled out, "the counselor told me some things. A lot of things, really. Stuff I didn't want to hear." I was babbling, but Billy let me. "He said, well, he said that I ought to take a look at my drinking." I paused.

Billy watched me carefully, saying nothing.

My throat felt like I'd swallowed a wad of cotton. I licked my lips and pushed on with it. "He didn't say I was an alcoholic, but he came damn close to it." The knot in my chest wouldn't let me take a deep breath. I sort of gasped, and the rest of it spilled out. "Billy, do you think I'm an alcoholic?"

I was afraid to breathe. Why had I asked Billy that stupid, stupid question? As soon as it was out of my mouth, he'd looked away from me. And who could blame him? Only a crazy person would ask somebody a question like that. The knot in my chest opened and spread its cold fingers. Everything inside me was as still and icy as the grave. I shivered as seconds seemed to stretch on the delicate silk of silence between us. Was he ever, I began to wonder, going to answer me? At last, he did. His voice was quiet. "Do you think you're an alcoholic?"

Disappointment fell on me. Why had Billy answered me with another question? He was supposed to be my witness for the defense. I'd banked on him to give a counter testimony that would wipe out the counselor's worrisome questions. But my witness had turned the tables. Now, I'd have to answer instead.

"Well, there are days when I don't drink at all." Yes, that was true. But there was more that I wasn't saying. Those were hangover days when my stomach twisted away from thoughts of liquor, and I suffered a tortuous thirst for water that gave me a churning nausea when I drank it. Even smoking cigarettes made me sick.

"I mean," I continued, deliberately not looking at Billy, "don't alcoholics have to drink every day? So, then, I wouldn't qualify. Would I?"

Billy gave me a penetrating look. "I can't answer that for you, Frankie. You're the one that would know."

For a ridiculously long moment, I felt like crying. Instead, I choked it back and said, "Well, thanks for listening to me." Now, it was me turning away.

"Frankie," Billy said.

"Yeah?" I half-turned, hoping that he didn't notice the tears standing in my eyes.

"If you wanna talk about this again. I, uh. Well, I always got time to listen. Right?"

"Right, Billy. Thanks a lot."

I picked up the drink he'd bought me and took it back to my seat. On the jukebox, Smokey Robinson crooned, *You really got a hold on me*, while I lifted the glass of scotch. I'd never particularly like that song. It was depressing. As I drank, I realized I really didn't like the taste of scotch. I put the glass down and stared into my drink. Random images flashed in memory: College. A movie date. Something about wine and roses. Jack Lemmon and Lee Remick drinking their way through marriage. Jack Lemon finally stopping after he goes to

Alcoholics Anonymous meetings. And Lee Remick unable to. In the end, I remembered, he leaves her.

I frowned at the two drinks in front of me. That movie wasn't like the ones I saw when I was growing up. In those, bars were romantic, exciting places where sleek, magnolia-skinned women—all done up in drop-dead black satin gowns, sporting layers of diamond bracelets—perched on stools drinking martinis out of stemmed, frosted glasses. Where were they, these sophisticated creatures who never drank too much? Did they turn into Lee Remick? Had I? Mentally, I shook myself. Why was I thinking about stupid movies? I pushed them out of my mind by lighting a cigarette and listening to Smokey again.

You really got a hold on me, he testified. Suddenly, I wanted to cry a bucket of tears. Maybe I'd take that counselor up on his offer. Just quit the stuff. I could do it. Couldn't I? I looked down at the glasses in front of me again. One was empty and ice was melting in the other. *Stop now!* Something said inside my brain. *Walk away from the stuff.* But could I? A thick, black cloud of fear swept into my heart.

Charlie stumbled up to the bar again. "Say, Frankie, you ready for another scotch, yet?"

I looked up at him and knew, deep down inside, that I was in bad trouble. As bad as can be. Because I couldn't keep myself from telling Charlie: "Sure, you know I never turn down a drink."

Predators

"Homosexuality is not a deviation; it is a variation. And people need to know that."

Peter J. Gomes, Minister

Allen's black and white television sat on a beer cooler in a corner behind the bar, and you couldn't really see it unless you were sitting almost on top of it. From where I usually sat at the bar, I could see it fine if it was on. Today it was, and I was watching Les build my drink when the *CBS Evening News* came on. The anchor, Walter Cronkite, always distinguished, always credible, opened with the story of the "Save Our Children" campaign. It had started a short while ago, Cronkite said, pausing to glance down at the sheaf of papers in his hand, with Anita Bryant and her organization pushing for Miami to repeal the city ordinance prohibiting discrimination against homosexuals.

As soon as the word homosexual rolled out of Cronkite's mouth in basso tones, everybody seemed to come to instant attention. I shifted my eyes away from Les to the television broadcast, feeling everything inside me go stock still, just like a rabbit that's caught the scent of danger in high grass.

Out of the corner of my eye, I could see Katie, the waitress, headed for the jukebox, but Cecil, sitting at a table behind me, stopped her.

"Wait up," he said. "I wanna hear the news." Katie shrugged and backed off.

That was unusual. Watching the news got very low priority even when there were only a handful of us at Allen's, so my nerve endings went on alert. Plus, I'd heard about Bryant's campaign. Which in itself was enough to get anxiety skipping through my veins. The campaign was getting a lot of national play and in Evansville, people were paying attention. At the very least, conversations gave it a passing nod if not full blown commentary. Not long ago, a man that I'd thought was open-minded and liberal had stunned me.

"Anita Bryant is right," he'd raged after I'd asked him what he thought about her campaign. "That scum should be hunted down and put in a concentration camp somewhere away from normal people." I particularly remembered his eyes while he'd said it. They'd gone hard and black and lightless. It was his eyes that had frightened me the most. He'd shown me his Mr. Hyde face, a part of him that I didn't know. And that part had drawn a line of separation in the sand with me standing one side and him on the other although he didn't know it. Didn't know about Stacey, about my woman dreams, about the real me I kept chained in secret corners. Nobody here did.

Glancing around, I realized that only a couple of familiar faces, the regulars that made Allen's so comfortable for me, were here today. Clyde, on the barstool in the corner and John, next to him. The rest— Cecil, Sonny, Nance, Gloria, and Betty—came in less often. As always Les was behind the bar and Katie was waiting tables, but there were a few others that I didn't know. For some reason, without the regulars that I knew so well, Allen's felt less cozy, less like home. Was there a chill in the air? I pulled my cardigan sweater closer around my chest.

On camera, Cronkite reminded us that aside from being a Miss America runner-up, Anita Bryant was best known as spokeswoman for Florida orange juice commercials. Bryant had gotten famous for telling the television audience, "A day without Florida orange juice is a day without sunshine."

Now, I thought to myself, she'd switched to selling something else. Something dark. I could hear aggravated murmurs from Cecil and the other guys sitting at his table. I drew in a ragged breath. Keeping up my camouflage was harder with Anita Bryant stirring things up. Where was my drink? I glanced at Les; he was moving in slow motion.

Cronkite went to a film clip of Bryant at a Midwestern news conference. A newsman asked about her motives for the campaign. Surrounded by microphones, the dark-haired, former beauty queen beamed at the camera and opened her mouth to oblige.

"Since homosexuals cannot reproduce," she said, striking a tone of both sincerity and loathing, "they must recruit children to freshen their ranks. We must not allow them to continue."

I clinched my fist, furious, thinking: *How can she get away with saying a pure lie like that?*

Somebody, a woman's voice, growled: "One of them mess wit my baby and he gonna get his ass kicked!"

I blew out a frustrated breath. What Bryant was saying boiled down to a load of crap. You didn't choose or get recruited like you were joining the army or some kind of club. You were born the way you were born.

I thought about Stacey and rubbed the palm of my hand across my lips. Nobody had recruited me into being attracted to women. Nobody had forced me to love her. That admission woke up The Corners, the place, at the back of my mind, where I'd vaulted my secrets. Like autumn leaves, they began to crackle and rustle. Which served to unnerve me even more than Anita Bryant. Mostly, I could keep them quiet and still as a tomb.

On screen, you could see the reporters scribbling furiously on their pads. Bryant was gabbing away, talking like she'd made some kind of a scientific study and was releasing the results.

It pissed me off that people put the rap on us for what pedophiles did. If you paid attention to your stats, or to what the neighborhood grapevine whispered about the husband down the street, you'd know that damn near all pedophiles were heterosexuals. To cover that up, folks muddied the water so that people would confuse pedophiles with homosexuals. But they weren't the same at all.

I paid attention to the screen again. Why wasn't somebody questioning Anita Bryant's claims? The reporters were just standing there, eating it up like starving animals. That was the scary part. I lit a cigarette and I dragged my hand across my lips again. When Les put my drink down in front of me, I almost knocked it over grabbing for it.

One reporter finally asked Bryant a question. He wanted to know how she chose the name for her campaign. She put one white hand to her neck and looked earnestly into the camera's eye.

"We chose the name because we want to save our children by stopping these homosexuals. They're predators!"

"Lock em all up!" Shouted an angry, male voice behind me.

I jumped involuntarily, taken aback by the fury in it.

Bryant continued in a tone filled with piety: "What they're doing is immoral and goes against God's wishes!"

I flushed with anger. *What a self-righteous ass! How can she claim to know what God wants?*

"Damn sissies!" Said another voice filled with disgust.

Cronkite switched to a sidebar news report that caught my attention. Last week, in a city where Anita Bryant had drawn a huge, unruly crowd, a teenaged boy believed to be a homosexual had been hospitalized after receiving a severe beating at his high school.

My bristling anger melted down into alarm, then, gradually, into dismay.

Yesterday, Cronkite continued, shortly after a local community rally in a different city where Bryant had been the speaker, two women thought to be Lesbians had been assaulted near a downtown bar by a group of men. But, Cronkite hastened to add, there was no direct evidence linking these acts of violence to Bryant's campaign against homosexuals.

By the time the sidebar ended, I felt like prey, trembling and ready to fly. Around the room, mutterings thickened the air. There was a mean edge in them.

"Serves they asses right!" Somebody near me said.

Cringing, I looked around to identify the voice. It was Nance. He'd come up behind me, and was leaning on the bar. I was suddenly, sharply aware that other people had come up to see the television better, and were standing close to me. Their nearness pressed down on my chest.

Standing next to me, Cecil growled, "Goddamn punks!" He decided to stir the pot. "Somebody oughta do us all a favor and wipe em all out!"

His tone made my hair stand on end. I could hear the mutterings in the room boiling up to higher temperatures. I'd never felt anything like this in Allen's before. Anita Bryant had raked up a kind of meanness, a kind of glad rush to violence that lay hidden underneath these people,

161

like my friend who'd changed from Dr. Jekyll to Mr. Hyde.

Suddenly, a chorus of voices rang out.

"Fags! I ain't got no use for'm!"

"A punk ain't worth shit!"

"Freaks!"

The venom in their voices shredded something inside me. The bar was humming with murmurs and curses. Near panic had me drain my glass and I held it up for Les to see I wanted another.

Cecil's pecan-colored face had gone shades darker with anger. "If I ever catch one around me again," he said in a deadly tone, "I'll cut his balls off!"

My armpits felt sweaty. With shaky fingers, I stubbed out my cigarette, remembering what I'd heard about Cecil. Rumor said that he'd beat the shit out of this harmless, little neighborhood guy that people said *looked like* he could be "that way." Supposedly, the little guy had said something that Cecil took as a come-on. Carrying a couple of hundred pounds and six feet of muscle, Cecil had the body to put a hurtin on you, and he'd fucked up the little guy really bad. Then, he'd bragged about it in Allen's for a week. He was a stony-hearted bastard if there ever was one.

Sonny, always an ass-hole, decided to jump in. He pitched his voice to get the attention of the crowd. "Man, what about those bull daggers? If you ask me, all those women need is a real man that knows how to lay the pipe right!" He laughed loud and hard. So did the other phallic egos standing around.

Fury sliced into my brain. I slammed my glass down on the bar and opened my mouth to speak, but a voice in my head whispered: *You'd better keep your mouth shut. Did you hear how they sounded? What do you think they'd do if they knew you were one of the freaks?*

162

That shut me down. I lit another cigarette and listened to the voice.

If you tell them who you are, you won't belong in here anymore. You won't belong anywhere in Evansville. Then what'll you do?

While I thought about that, at the back of my eyes, I could see myself standing in the yard of the loneliest place on earth. Just for a moment, I was a kid, back again at the Alcoa House, waiting and desperately hoping for my parents to come and get me, waiting and listening to the sound of evening crickets—a sound to hollow out a place in your heart and fill it with stinging tears.

The voice spoke again: *You won't belong. Then what'll you do?*

I tasted bile on my tongue, but I swallowed it. Swallowed and pressed my lips together. Shivers touched my shoulders like icy fingertips. I couldn't imagine. Didn't dare imagine the loneliness of not belonging. Cold dread burrowed into me and found a home. For warmth, I hunched over my empty glass. Looking down into it, I saw myself there, and saw, rising up before me, a coiling, twisting mass of shadows, swaying as if it would strike.

Around the room, edges of evening darkness had stolen quietly through Allen's windows while angry, clamoring voices filled the air with gathering clouds. Near my hand, a weak, ragged patch of November light lay dying on the bar.

It was autumn's end. And, winter was coming.

Part Three: Tribes

Los Angeles, California

Almost everyone seeks a sense of belonging

John J. Macionis

Once you know who you are, you don't have to worry any more.

Nikki Giovanni

Tribes

Tribe: a family, esp. a large one.

Webster's Dictionary

"...and chile, they say he's telling everybody he's Gay!" Declared a man's voice dripping with scandal and reproach.

My head swiveled to the left and I stared at the three young, Black guys hunched over drinks at the corner of the bar. I could clearly hear every word they were saying because it was always relatively empty in Jewel's Room on Saturday afternoons. Only a handful of people were at tables that sat at the edge of the dance floor.

"You tellin tales, Miss Thing. Ain't no way one of our Black preachers gonna admit to that!" Said a second voice, clearly shocked and tickled pink about it.

They sounded like women gossiping over the back fence although they didn't look like it; all three looked like poster boys for football's hall of fame.

"Well, he is! Can you believe it, a preacher saying he's Gay? From the pulpit?" Asked Scandalized, his voice rising for the sake of drama.

Like most bars, Jewel's Room was the site of much gossip, intrigue, and signifying. It was the main Black Gay bar in Los Angeles and what you heard here was usually provocative.

The third man in the trio, whose body language told you he was straight as an arrow, said: "I'm appalled. How could you admit to being Gay in public these days? This is 1987. It's getting ugly out there with people saying we're spreading some kind of disease. Who the hell is this man?"

One of the bartenders on duty, a teeny-tiny woman who always seemed to know more dirt than a Hollywood gossip columnist, was huddled with them. "I know Carl," she confided while she polished shot glasses. "Knew em back in New York when he was with The Bradford Singers on Broadway."

"Huhn! One of those Broadway divas, I might have known," said Tickled Pink. He had a Hollywood handsome face.

"Tell us more, dear!" said Straight as an Arrow.

The bartender moved closer and dropped her voice to comply, so I couldn't hear the rest. News about what was going on, "in the life" and otherwise, in L.A. came through Jewel's faster than a speeding bullet. Since I'd been living here, I'd learned that unless you're plugged into some kind of network in Los Angeles, you don't know what's going on in this giant beehive. In the last six years that I'd struggled to make a nest here, I'd been out of the loop and disconnected until seven months ago when I'd found Jewel's.

"Psst, Henry!" I called to the other bartender, the one closest to me. He switched over. The color of butternut squash and slender as a willow, Henry didn't have the come-hither body of an Adonis, but he loved to roll his hips as if he did when he walked. The walk, he'd told me in all sincerity with a bit of drama thrown in for effect, was an essential part of his "glorious personae as a queen." I had figured out that Henry wasn't what they called flaming, but he was close enough so that he couldn't pass for straight even if he'd wanted to. It was clear, however, that he did not.

"Another scotch?" Henry asked when he was facing me.

"Not now. I want to know who they're talkin about down there." I nodded in the three musketeers' direction.

"The new Black preacher in town. He's Gay and he's out. They say he's starting a church named Unity Fellowship of Christ especially for The Children, and he's telling them when they come, they don't have to be in the closet."

"Whaat?" I was momentarily silenced by such daring. And fatally intrigued. A move like that smacked of bold non-conformity. A thing dear to my heart.

"What's his name, Henry?"

"They said it's Reverend Carl Bean."

In Black talk, whether Gay or not, when you heard somebody referencing the almighty *they*, you knew it was shorthand for The Grapevine, the fastest messaging system in the known world. Sometimes, what *they* said was gospel truth; sometimes, it was straight-up lies. Sometimes, it fell somewhere in between.

Before I knew it was going to happen, a string of questions popped out of my mouth. "Where's the church? What street? What time?"

Henry was wiping the bar. "I don't know. Let me check with the girls down there." He grinned devilishly at the label he'd given them.

I goggled at him, a little shocked at his calling them girls outright. Wasn't that an insult? Some gay men didn't like it if you implied they were feminine in any way. Since I was still new on the block, so to speak, I wasn't quite sure about how to take things people said at Jewel's. Coded language, I was used to. Black folks had always used coded language so that White people couldn't understand what we were talking about, but The Children spoke code that was even more cryptic. This was a different world. And I was still learning my A B C's.

Suddenly, music blasted out of the jukebox as Jimmy Jam and his partner, Terry, hit the opening licks for Janet Jackson's "Control." It brought back memories of the first night I'd come to Jewel's. Bass rhythms had been rolling through the room like tidal waves. A flickering strobe light caught the exaggerated poses of the dancers, so that they resembled a still life study as they moved like metronomes to the music's pulse—heads bobbing, bodies swaying, arms dipping in perfect sync to Janet's beat.

And I'd been dazzled. Not by the dancers, mind you, or the music. But by the same-sex couples everywhere I looked: On the lighted stairway going up to the next level, lolling against the rose-colored walls, roosting on barstools, vibrating on the dance floor. Women with women. Men with men. I'd been dazzled because I'd never been in a public space before where you could congregate and be who you were without fear of discovery. A girl-girl couple passed by, stopping, for a moment, to kiss each other full on the lips. Their open intimacy with each other had me gaping. Near me, at a table, a quartet of men eyed each other outright as they laughed and shouted over the music. As if on cue, I heard Janet declare: *I do what's right for me,* while the percussionist steadily kept the backbeat. I felt dumbstruck and in awe of these people. Never had I seen anything like this.

I ordered a drink and, out of the shadows, a woman emerged. The sharp contrast of her precisely cut, white pants suit against her skin's soft blackness drew my eyes to her. As she flowed through the crowd, something about her beckoned other women, and they positioned themselves, like sweet temptations, in her path. When she neared, they stepped close, smiled, touched her arm, and leaned provocatively into her space. I watched, fascinated. She was a lodestone woman. A magnet. *Like Stacey,* something in me whispered. Eventually, the woman in white stopped at an empty bar stool next to mine and ordered a beer. While she stood waiting for it, I desperately wanted to ask her name, but shyness kept me silent.

I smiled remembering that night. I'd never found out who the woman in white was. And though I always looked for her when I came, I'd never seen her again. If I ever did, maybe, I'd have the nerve to speak to her.

I'm in control, Janet sang. *Control... control... control....* The word echoed again and again as the song ended.

I glanced down the bar at Henry. He was busy cackling with the musketeers. I took a sip of scotch and lit a cigarette as the jukebox came to life again. *Ohh, I wanna dance with somebody,* Whitney Houston wailed, and two guys wearing running suits followed each other to the dance floor. For a few minutes, they had the spotlight to themselves, dancing with racing energy, as if they were sprinters going for the finish line. Then, a tall, busty woman, dressed in jeans, escorted a woman in a skirt and boots to the floor.

The women began to do a smooth, updated version of the Jitterbug, and as they did, my mind kicked backwards to my obsession, in the tenth grade, with Dick Clark's *American Bandstand*; it was the television show I'd raced home every day to see. I'd call Judy and we'd talk as we watched blonde Justine, dark-haired Mike, the two Carols, and all the rest of the regulars take to the dance floor. Our conversation was all about who danced the best, the outfits the girls were wearing, which couple was the cutest, the records we liked, and all the other things teenagers talk about. Growing up things.

On Jewel's dance floor, the guys were doing The Snake like keyed up dynamos while Whitney insisted that she wanted to feel the heat with somebody. The Snake was a dance I hadn't managed to master, so I watched them, trying to figure out what I was doing wrong. As I did, I flashed back to seventh grade and teaching myself how to do the Jitterbug by watching Acey Boy's dance show for local Black kids on television. It had been hard to teach myself, but I'd managed it because I'd watched other people for a long time. It was important to me to be able to fit in, to be able to dance when the d.j. played "Rockin Robin" or "Jim Dandy to the Rescue" at the dances in Vine Junior High's gym after basketball games.

When you're growing up, that's the way you learn. By imitating others, like you, in public places. You watch. You copy them. You learn how to dance. How to act. I was watching the couples on Jewel's dance floor, but in my mind's eye, I saw myself in Vine Junior's gym with Russell, Sammie, Bernie, Calvin, and all the sweating boys standing in a bunch on one side while, on the other side, us nervous girls waited for one of them to take that long walk across the floor, hold out a hand, and ask one of us for a dance. It was the same ritual every time. One boy broke the ice, then the rest followed suit.

Following suit is one way you get schooled about the rules of engagement with the opposite sex. I put my cigarette out, thinking back. In Evansville, at Allen's bar, where I was busy blending in with the crowd, I'd been bold because I knew the moves in the boy-meets-girl game. And I'd played the game to keep my camouflage tight. To survive. Here at Jewel's, the moves were new to me and I'd been shy with the woman in white because I'd felt like a know-nothing. Like I was back at Vine Junior in the shoes of the sweating boys, trying to figure out what to do next. Whatever the moves for girl-meets-girl were, I didn't know because I hadn't been schooled for it. Even though, I'd been with Stacey and a few other women before I'd found Jewel's, it had all been secret. That meant the moves were different—indirect and obscure, not like the ones you'd make in a place where you could be open. You danced a different dance in secret.

On the floor, Busty woman and her partner moved together like Fred and Ginger, weaving The Jitterbug into The Walk in sure-footed patterns that made it all look easy as pie. The guys doing The Snake were good, too, but there was something about the way they moved that reminded me of two puppets being jerked up and down by an unseen hand.

I thought about Stacey and me. Years had passed since those days in college. Together in secret, we'd lived in a bottle. Adrift. Without a tribe to give us aid and comfort. For us, there'd been nobody to compare notes with. Nobody to ask advice from. Nobody to teach us. No way to learn how to be who we were without shame. Was that why we didn't make it? I wondered. Why fear had gotten a toehold and eaten us up? All of a sudden, I felt cheated because, I realized, that in all of my life, there'd been no public spaces where it was safe to take off my camouflage, where it was safe to watch and learn. Straight people took those things for granted, but we were deprived of them. Something heavy settled on my shoulders as I thought about what we had missed. What we were denied. And what that had cost us. Cost me.

I looked over at Henry again, thinking about what he'd told me about this new church. Would it be a safe space, too, like Jewel's? Some place warm where you gathered for comfort with others like you around the campfire? Maybe. But there was a strange reluctance in me to find out.

Henry was hip-rolling his way back to me. He looked like Mae West. Or Lucy Ricardo imitating Mae West. I couldn't decide which. Either way it was hilarious. I chuckled to myself.

When he reached me he rolled his eyes toward the musketeers and said, "I asked the girls. Church starts at

11:30 at the Ebony Showcase over on Washington, near Rimpau. You going?"

I shrugged. "Might." And I stared down into my empty glass, trying to make up my mind. Curiosity nudged me to go. After all, I wasn't doing a damn thing on Sunday mornings except pouring myself a glass of mother scotch while I watched Terri Cole Whittaker preach wealth and abundance.

The cynic in me put in a word. *Why bother?* It asked. *This church won't be any different than the rest you've tried.*

Nobody knew but me that after years of searching, I'd finally given up on finding a church and a preacher that could move something inside me. Resigned to that, I was reluctant to get my hopes up again for nothing.

I watched Henry moving about. He was in his glory. No camouflage for him. I wondered how he'd managed to survive like that. Camouflaging had been the only way I'd known. The first maxim had been: Stay in the shadows. And don't show yourself to other people—not even to others like you. This new preacher was going against all that. Like Henry, he was putting himself out there for everybody to see. Which was why he intrigued me. He was breaking all the rules, going against all I'd learned to do. And that was fascinating. Exciting.

The little rebel that lived inside me peeked out, right then, and tugged at my sleeve.

What the hell, it whispered. *Let's go see what this preacher is about.*

And that's all it took.

Sanctuary

Sanctuary: A building set aside for worship. A holy place. Asylum of safety and security. Place of refuge or protection. A Christian church. Reservation where animals or birds are sheltered and may not be hunted or trapped.

Webster's Dictionary

1. The Ebony Showcase

My first time going to church at Unity Fellowship Church of Christ was in 1987 when services were being held at the Ebony Showcase Theater; the Ebony was an old girl whose days of glitz and glamour had passed. She sat on Washington Boulevard, near the corner of Rimpau; I found her without any trouble because she sported an old-fashioned marquee, topped off with a vertical sign announcing her name in fancy letters. When you walked into the lobby, you could tell she had been a queen, but her reign had ended and that she had fallen on hard times. In the theater, the seats had been upholstered in a rich, red; now, you had to be careful of which seat you chose because, on some seats, the faded, red upholstery was so worn that the nails might snag your clothes. In bygone days, the wall color, now faint and dull, had been a deep, rich hue, accented with gilded wall sconces that, over the years, had tarnished. The roof must have had holes in it because, overhead, I could hear the sound of bird wings. Pigeons had somehow gotten in and were roosting there in the rafters. We could hear them cooing and could see them flapping around the ceiling. On either side of the stage, red velvet curtains hung, showing threadbare patches here and there. There was a small podium and although somebody had rolled a piano on stage, there was no choir. Back then, there wasn't even a person to play the piano.

I'd come out of curiosity. Fascination, really, with what I'd heard about the man who'd had the nerve, the courage, to be a minister as an openly Gay man in the heart of the Black Los Angeles. Reverend Carl Bean had put the word out that he was starting a church where you didn't have to be in the closet. Where you could be out. Be openly who you were. Doing that went against the social grain in a very big way and I sensed a sea change in that message. Sensed the presence of something that I'd looked for in a church and had never found. And so, I came.

The first time I went I saw about two dozen people, some of whom I recognized from Jewel's Room. There was a tentative feel about being in this new church. As if we were all waiting for some dramatic something to jump off. Which was not surprising since a lot of us drew breath, I'd noticed, as if we were living our lives inside a soap opera. But there was nothing dramatic that occurred. Only a quiet sense, for me, of coming home. A feeling that would draw me back again and again.

On Sundays, I'd always sit in the back, a vantage point that let me see the others coming in. Sitting in the back also gave me full view of whoever got up to speak during Testimony. Which took place before the service actually began. The same woman usually led it each Sunday. It was pretty informal. She'd simply stand down in front of the stage and ask who wanted to talk about what was happening with them. During Testimony, Reverend Bean would stand near the stage's left wing, listening to what the people were saying. A short, stocky man with luminous eyes in a walnut brown face, he always wore a plain, black robe that looked more like a graduation gown than one of those fancy, big-sleeved, velvet-trimmed outfits that preachers usually favored.

I had to get used to Testimony over time. The first Sunday I'd come, this part of the service had completely taken me aback. People standing up and talking about very personal things like: "I lost my job," or "My lover left me," or "My rent money is runnin funny"—that kind of honesty went directly against the ironclad rule I'd been taught back home in Knoxville. "Never tell your business. Especially to strangers." Those rules, I began to understand, didn't apply at Unity. Camouflaging and making myself invisible were old ways that I'd learned to survive, but I'd paid a high price to use them. Here, it was about finding common ground to build on. About telling the truth. About talk that reveals rather than hides. It was about learning to trust the connection you were building with other people. It was about something entirely different than what I'd experienced at other churches.

2. Affirmation

Having been told over and over again that we had been excommunicated, not just from church, but from God, most of us came into Unity feeling trapped. Threatened. Lost. Like animals being hunted into extinction. Or untouchables banished into the artic wilderness.

Reverend Bean understood that and so, at the beginning of Unity's service every Sunday morning, he spoke words of Affirmation. It was, I began to understand, after a time, a ritual act of healing with words. He would dim the lights and ask us to close our eyes. Then he would say:

"Wherever you identify yourself sexually along God's rainbow, know that you are not in error. You are God's creation. You are not a mistake. Homosexual, Lesbian, Transgender, Heterosexual, Bisexual. God made you the way you are. And God loves you just the way you are. So love yourself and know that you are very special!"

It was so strange to hear it. To take it in. To let it become a part of us. Because we'd been told, over and over again, that we were freaks of nature, an abomination, the snot in God's nostrils. They had preached at us that God, and all good people who loved God, hated us. But now, now, someone had come to tell us the opposite.

"God loves you just the way you are."

Having someone affirm me out loud Sunday after Sunday gradually began to change the shape and substance of reality for me.

"You are not in error."

Listening to those words, to that Affirmation, changed not only the mirror that I looked into, but what I saw there.

"You are not a mistake. You are God's creation. So love yourself."

In West Africa, the Dogon people of Mali have an expression which means the mighty power of the word: *Nommo*. They believe in the magic power of the word. The power of words to transform. *Nommo*.

Sunday after Sunday, I listened to the Affirmation. The words were healing me. Changing me. Sunday after Sunday, its power worked. *Nommo*. The mighty power of the word. One day, I looked into the mirror and found it was no longer cracked. One day, I looked into the mirror and the image it showed me was whole. *Nommo*.

3. The Welcome Table

Sometimes, during Unity's service, I thought about Auntie's version of God. When she was babysitting me, she would listen to radio services, sitting in her rocking chair in her living room, with the *Bible* open on her lap. I was required to sit with her and listen. On the radio, the southern White preachers would rant and rave about sin and sinners, sounding like maniacs possessed.

"Come to Jee-suz!" They would suddenly holler, scaring me half to death. "He'll wash away your sinss-zuh!"

These preachers and others, my own included, seemed to be practicing a religion awash with sinners who were always being threatened, judged, and condemned, and who were constantly being exhorted and cajoled into following a path to salvation. Nobody seemed to want to follow it; you had to be pushed into it, like a stubborn mule. Which, to me, made their path to salvation seem a depressing prison sentence, something to be served out and endured, or, worse, a grim torment that required you to suffer in guilt-ridden martyrdom. There was a catch to this kind of religion though. You had to "prove" you were worthy to be saved. Preachers and church saints made it clear that not everybody was worthy. Only some got chosen. *Does God discriminate?* I wondered back then. Now, I knew it was people who did that. Did it and put the rap on God.

At Unity, the motto that "God is Love and Love is for Everyone" attracted a lot of folks, not just Black people and not just Gay people. Reverend Bean had chosen that motto because God, according a verse in scripture, has no respect of persons. In other words, you didn't have to prove you were worthy since everybody has an open invitation to the welcome table. God, I learned at Unity, wasn't into the discriminating business.

Unfortunately, that was not so for people, by and large. By the late 1980's, there was a new kind of discrimination. And a new kind of oppression brought on by a virus. AIDS. In the beginning, it ravaged Gay men, becoming the mark of Cain and a new kind of leprosy. You were shunned if you had it. You languished alone in hospital beds, mostly unattended by frightened nurses and bewildered doctors. Or you suffered alone at home—too devastated to tell anybody, too ashamed to admit that you'd got it. And chances were, you died alone, in the grip of a merciless affliction that wasted you to skin and bones.

AIDS. No communities of color stepped up, in the beginning, to fight it and no Black churches would touch it. Reverend Bean was the first to take it on with Unity, and its outreach arm, Minority AIDS Project welcoming, hugging, and helping those who were ill. We advocated. Demonstrated. Educated. Visited. Shopped. Cooked. Nursed. Cleaned. We stayed to hold their hands. Right through to the end. Stayed to bury, to remember. To celebrate the going home. Because others wouldn't.

AIDS. It would set Unity apart. And it would change my life.

4. The Bible

By 1989, Unity had moved to 5149 Jefferson Boulevard, into the big space that, during the week, became the lobby of Minority AIDS Project. The word had gotten out and, most Sundays, it was Standing Room Only at church. If you came late, there'd be no more seats and you'd be standing around the walls, or listening out in the hallway which led back to the offices. In the area that served as a pulpit, there were proper chairs and a podium for Reverend Bean and our assistant pastor, Reverend Zach and about two dozen folding chairs to seat our choir, the Voices of Unity, officially robed in wine and rose. Near them, and almost out of sight, there was a piano in the corner. This one, our choir director, Darren McCarroll-Jones, played like nobody's business each Sunday.

Song was an old African and, eventually, African-American way of healing. Of unbinding. Song freed us from the worries, the uncertainties, the torments. You could fly away home on a song. Every Sunday, the choir sang and we joined in, singing to lift our wings. And fly.

I don't know what you came to do, the lead singer's voice would ring out.

And the other choir voices would answer: *I came to shout for Jesus.*

They would gather the song in their throats and hurl it out to the rest of us and we would stand to catch it, mold it, sanctify it with hands clapping, heads nodding, bodies swaying under its galvanizing power. As Darren's fingers flew across the piano keys, waves of emotion, tidal and mighty, would rush through the church, building until the church moved, alive with what Reverend Bean called the Holy Ghost. Song was deliverance. Unshackling in its power. Suddenly, you'd see a man leap out of his seat, crashing over chairs, pushing aside people's confining hands, so he could sprint around the aisles. Then, across the room, the Holy Spirit, like a whirling tornado, would catch hold of a Transgender woman and she would hop out of the front row holy-dancing in spike heels all the way to the back of the church. Some would rock and weep; some would dance in place, stiffen, and topple straight back, like felled trees, into waiting arms. Others just jumped for joy while male and female ushers would rush hither and thither, passing out Kleenex and wooden-handled fans.

After the music ministry, it was "study time," as Reverend Bean would call his sermons. He'd tell us to get out our *Bibles* so we could go to work. We were all, in our own individual ways, captives. In chains. Beaten up and terrorized. But Reverend Bean told us we couldn't really be free of oppression's chains just through dancing and singing. We had to, he showed us, confront the thing that preachers had used to terrorize us: *The Bible.*

It didn't matter whether some of us had been Methodists, like me, or Baptist, like Reverend Bean, or Apostolic, or A.M.E. or Presbyterian or Catholic. We'd all been bullied, brainwashed, and beaten up. And the *Bible* had been the tool people had used to demonize us, scare us to death, and keep us under control—no matter whether it was because we were people of color, or women, or same gender attracted.

We'd been clueless that its books had been compiled, censored, and used by people who wanted to control and exclude folks from the welcome table. A case in point, Reverend Bean reminded us, was how certain verses in the *Bible* were used to justify keeping us Black people as slaves. "Like anything else," he said, "you can use things in the *Bible* for good or ill. "

"Don't be intimidated by this book," Rev would say to us, holding up his *Bible,* realizing that we were clearly terrified of it. "It's sixty-six books all written by different people who saw and understood the world within the limited knowledge of their own cultures and time."

Well. That was an eye-opener. Different people? Not God? I could see Auntie spinning in her fundamentalist grave.

In one of his teaching sermons, Reverend Bean tackled the two creation stories in Genesis which, he showed us, had obviously been written by two different authors who wrote in two different styles. We were amazed as he went through them and pointed out the differences.

Using the *Bible* to further bigotry and oppression had started a long time ago, we found out. With red ink, margin notes scribbled all over his *Bible*, Rev would come out from behind the podium and walk between the rows of chairs where we sat. He wasn't just preaching; he was teaching, giving us permission to really think about the book that we were studying.

"You have to read the *Bible* for yourself," he'd admonish us. "You have to think," he'd say. "You have the right to interpret, to ask questions."

When Rev turned to the story of "Sodom and Gomorrah," everybody trembled in their boots. This was the tale most used by preachers to put us Gay folks on trial and condemn us to the torments of hell. Reverend Bean deconstructed the story and dispatched our fear of it, going through the verses, line by line, careful to include historical and cultural information for clarification. He emphasized that the word "know" in that story is typically translated using a connotative interpretation that implies sexual intimacy and he told us that it wasn't uncommon for words in the Bible to be misinterpreted in translation. Perhaps deliberately. For "Sodom and Gomorrah" is, basically, not a story about homosexuals on the rampage, but a story about the importance of hospitality in desert cultures, about their xenophobic suspicion of strangers, and about how women were commonly used as placating sex objects.

Reverend Bean's gifts as a teacher and forthright boldness in the pulpit was a wonder to me. What Reverend Bean was doing on Sundays was waking us up— liberating us from double-tongued ideas that had oppressed us, then put us to sleep. But then oppression can only work on the sleepers. On people who don't know or don't want to know what's going on.

Week after week, I kept coming back, thirsty to learn, ready to go beyond the limits and boundaries that Auntie's kind of religion imposed. Study time at Unity was about Liberation Theology. About freeing people from oppression and injustice. About giving you new wine in new bottles. Not about follow-the-leader, without thinking on your own.

Jesus of Nazareth, that radical thinker and liberationist, had done the same when he'd questioned the "Hebrew Scriptures." He'd gone around fighting oppression and injustice, wandered about giving people new ideas, gone about changing water into new wine and putting it in new bottles. That new wine, eventually, became some of the books of the "New Testament."

5. The Pigeons

When I think back to those days at the Ebony, I always remember the sound of flapping wings. The wings of pigeons flying overhead. They'd gotten in somehow and there they'd be—flapping frantically against the ceiling, bewildered at being trapped inside.

The pigeons. Maybe they were a sign. Because, in a way, we were like them—bewildered and desperate. Trapped inside a sexual identity that others despised. Each of us came to Unity looking for something. For asylum. For refuge. For deliverance. Like the pigeons, we had been flying frantically here and there—for all of our lives, really—flapping and bumping, lost and looking for a place we could simply be free. Like the pigeons over our heads, searching to get out, we, too, came searching. But our search was for a way in—to freedom, to peace. A way in: To sanctuary.

Skirmishes

The noon meeting of Alcoholics Anonymous in South Central Los Angeles was bedlam, as usual. As you came up the steps, noise greeted you first. The rising and falling babble, the heavy, shuffling footfalls, the clicking, castanet sound of high heels, the scuffing and scraping of metal chairs on the wooden floor. Noise. And then, you waded into a shifting kaleidoscope of people, Black, Brown, White. They were everywhere—so many that they threatened to overflow the walls of the mid-sized, second-floor room. People lingered at the entrance; people talked in bunches near the door; people stood inside; people sat in rows of folding chairs; they were smoking, eating doughnuts, and drinking coffee, waiting for the meeting to start. Overhead, cigarette smoke swirled thick as fog. Young mothers scrambled after screaming toddlers, men trudged to the back, headed for the super-sized coffee pot on the counter, and groups of newcomers, seated on the front row, whispered to each other and their sponsors.

In front of a picture window, up front, sat the leader's desk and beside it stood a podium, edged with small, white, Christmas lights that blinked on and off. In a corner, there was a small evergreen tree, waiting to be dressed.

Today, as I weaved through the moving people toward the front row, anxiety and confusion reigned supreme in my head. Cup of coffee in hand, I took my seat and tucked my legs under me before glancing up at the podium. A woman in glittering earrings was there reading. Instead of focusing on her, my mind raced this way and that, gnawing, like a dog with a bone, on my undoing a couple of hours ago. *How could this have happened?* My mind worried. *What am I gonna do?*

I tugged my focus back to the woman reading at the podium and part of a sentence filtered through my brain. "—admitted we were alcoholic," I heard her say.

And a memory burst into my field of view. I saw me, six months ago, standing in this room, admitting myself an alcoholic out aloud. That June day when I'd said those words, I'd felt as if a cloak of iron had suddenly fallen away from my shoulders. Almost immediately, everything brightened, just as if someone had turned on a light behind my eyes or thrown back thick curtains blocking my view. That was then. Right now, things didn't look so bright to me.

A screaming howl from somebody's baby startled me. I looked around and saw the baby's young mother a couple of rows away from me. Frazzled-looking as I felt, she rocked and bounced the howling bundle frantically, then shoved a bottle into the baby's mouth. If you didn't have a babysitter, you dragged your kid to the meeting. "Take yourself to meetings," they told us, "like you took yourself to the bar and to the liquor store." Meetings had to come first, before anything and everything else. I didn't want to drink again, so I followed the suggestions. But sometimes, things happened. Like today. Things that, meetings or no meetings, made you want to take a drink.

I glanced the faces around me. I knew I was like them: An alcoholic, desperately struggling to stay sober, but plagued by an allergy and an obsession to drink my way into the grave.

"Why can't you just stop?" Nita had asked me back in Evansville after watching me drink myself under the table one afternoon. "Why can't you make up your mind to just stop after five or six drinks?" Her brown eyes were earnest and full of concern. "Sip some water. Eat some Beer Nuts," she'd suggested, making it all sound so simple.

And I had tried. More than once. After drink number five, the first time. After drink number two, the next. Neither experiment worked. I figured it was what I was drinking that got me in trouble. And so, the third time, I'd tried with one glass of white wine. One glass of wine. Not one glass of scotch. Not one martini. Just wine. How hard could it be? Harder, I found out, than I could imagine. As hard as crossing the Sahara without water. One glass led to another, and another, which, then, led to a scotch or three, and before I knew it, I was blasted. *Why?* I'd asked myself in despair. *Why can't I do what Nita suggested?* I'd asked myself so many times after that.

The first week in these rooms, Sam's pitch had told me why. "It's the first one," he'd said. "That's the one that got me drunk. That's the one that gets us all drunk. For us, one is one too many."

Nobody understood that saying the way another alcoholic did. Nobody. If you listened to our stories for the similarities, not the differences, you'd discover that the road we'd all traveled had come out the same: First, it was fun, the drinking. Then, it began to sour and you found yourself on the chase, looking to reach the perfect high again, the one that you thought you'd reached once before, the one that would fix it all, forever and ever. The thing was, you never found it again if you'd ever found it in the first place, and the chase was becoming a grind now, something that was more work than fun. Then, came the day that you wanted to be shut of it all. Hang up your drinking glass, so to speak, and retire to a little coffee and tea with maybe a beer or a cocktail every now and then. And you tried to do it, but, by now, alcohol was on you like Tar Baby, and you couldn't shake it. The more you strained to break free, the tighter alcohol bound you. Until, one day, you knew. You knew it was not going to let you go. Not ever. And you figured you'd die that way, holding on to the bottle and the bottle holding on to you. Sometimes, I still wasn't all that sure that I wouldn't end up that way even though I was in twelve step now. Staying sober—learning how to live without liquor, without the reflex habit of it, without its false sense of protection—was monstrously hard. Billy had said so fifteen years ago in Allen's Lounge. He hadn't lied.

The woman with the glittering earrings had finished reading and the leader, a silver-haired White man, whose eyes said-don't-mess-with-me-today, looked around before calling somebody to come up next. I tried to shrink in my seat, praying he wouldn't call on me. Sharing at the podium scared me; so far, I'd never put my hand up on my own, and I'd never volunteered to share although, a couple of times, I'd been called on to do it. The leader pointed at a young brother seated a couple of rows back from me; the brother got up, making his way, in slow time, to the front.

Relieved, I lit a cigarette just as, out of the blue, an ambush thought dropped into my head: *A drink would be just the ticket right about now, wouldn't it? A scotch on the rocks to take the edge off, or a cold, three-olive, very-dry martini sliding down your throat would...*

Reluctantly, I pushed the half-finished thought away. Rear action thoughts like that scared me shitless. Sometimes they bombarded me like a blitz. Other times, they scaled my walls and sniped at me. I never knew when the hell the skirmishes would start. Or end. I looked down at my fingers. Temptation had them trembling, ever so slightly, like autumn leaves shiver when a cold breeze slithers by. I looked at the coffee in my hand, half-wishing that it was scotch or gin, and took a sip. It tasted like Mississippi mud.

At the podium, the young brother kept his head down. It was no wonder. His face looked like somebody had tossed him out of a window last night. I wondered if somebody had. His reading voice scaled up peaks, but mostly dropped down into valleys. I could barely hear him. "—is the desire to stay sober," he croaked.

Wanting to stay sober is one thing, I thought to myself as I listened to him. *Living it is another.*

True enough, nobody had promised a rose garden, but they didn't say anything about the part where everything, big and small, made me feel like I was hanging by my fingernails. Which kept me overwhelmed, tense, and tired. It was no walk in the park, this sobriety thing. Land mines were buried beneath the soil everywhere. Step wrong and you'd blow yourself up. Even your own thoughts were out to ambush you. I sighed. Why was it so hard?

My chest quivered as I breathed out. Alcohol had dulled my feelings most of the time. Had kept them mostly numb and asleep. Now, fears of every stripe and hue dogged me each and every second. Getting through the day sober was like inching forward in thick fog while I fought for balance on a rickety bridge that stretched across a deep gorge. Every waking moment, I kept blindly grabbing and clutching for a hold, kept sticking out my toe to feel the way, and always, always being terrified of losing my balance, of falling head over heel into the shadows below. Right now, the shadows felt very close—just a breath away. This morning, I'd gotten fired from my teaching job.

A rising hum of conversation coming from the back of the room threatened to drown out the ragged pitch of the brother's reading voice. The leader banged sharply on the desk for quiet and some people lowered their voices; others shut up altogether.

My head cranked out some the film of this morning's demoralizing calamity. Mortified about being fired and not wanting to be seen by anybody at the school, I'd hurried out of the building to the parking lot on Fifth Street.

At my car door, I'd heard a seductive thought whispering in my left ear: *You could go to Roscoe's have some chicken, have some waffles, and while you're waiting for the food, have a scotch on the rocks to calm your nerves. You deserve it!*

On the tail end of it, the sober part of my brain had gotten an SOS through: *Call your sponsor!* It had screamed and kept nagging me until I'd found a pay phone and dialed her up.

She had listened patiently to my hysterical ranting, then told me: "Don't drink. Get to the noon meeting. I'll be late getting there but wait for me."

So here I was. Following her orders. Though part of my mind kept longing for a cozy restaurant where they served waffles, fried chicken, and mother scotch, if you wanted it, on the side.

There was another woman, dressed in red sweats, at the podium now. I knew her. She'd relapsed and, two weeks ago, made it back to the rooms. The wear and tear of five months out there showed on her: Eyes puffy, tufts of dry, broken-off hair slicked down with too much hair grease, a sickly sheen to her walnut skin, the red sweats just a wee bit soiled and tattered. Looking at her, at any of the relapsers, gave me the willies. They'd gone out and had one more for the road. *Would I? Could I?* I wondered now.

One of the monkeys whispered: *It would be so easy. Such a simple thing, just get up. Go around the corner to The*

Flying Fox. It's easy enough to order up one for the road.
Mesmerized with the idea, my butt was a couple of inches off the seat when I thought about Marcie. That's when I caught myself and sat down.

Marcie was an old-timer who liked to remind everybody that she had more than twenty years sober, and that she'd seen a lot of folks go out, but precious few come back. Marcie—a petite redhead with freckles—had a savagely amusing way of describing the relapsers who made it back. She called them scouts. "Scouts," she'd say, in a tone spiked with irony, "go out and check the lay of the land. They be thinkin they can go back out there, and come out on top."

Each time I'd heard her say it, my head drew a picture of a horse with the relapser astride it dressed in buckskin and a cowboy hat, galloping out into the barren landscape, liquor bottle in hand, ready to do ferocious battle.

Fully enjoying her own spiel calculated to warn us against even thinking about going out, Marcie would say: "When alcohol finish whuppin they asses, they crawl back in here, if they lucky, with a butt full of arrows. You better know alcohol out there seriously kickin some ass." She'd pause for a moment, giving us a hard scowl. Then, she'd go back at it: "You go on out there if you want to. Just go on! Me? I'll be sittin right here! I got my ass kicked enough the first time around. Out there, alcohol be stone waitin on us to come on back for another round. And it ain't takin no prisoners."

At that, the room would laugh. But there was an uneasiness beneath it. What Marcie said was funny because she had a way with words, but there was nothing funny about the message. It was a straight-up warning. Any one of us could go out. We knew that. And we knew that if we did go, we might not make it back. A whole lot of us had died out there having one more. And that was plain scary.

Just like my drinking dreams were scary. Where, once, scotch had been my Linus blanket, now it was my own personal boogey man who had the leading role in my nightmares. In them, I watched myself putting the glass of mother scotch to my lips, smelling its fumes, struggling not to, but finally surrendering as I tipped the glass up, and let the scotch fall into my mouth.

The first time I had the dream, I woke in a cold sweat and called my sponsor, panicked. What did it mean? Was I going to drink again? She'd assured me that almost everybody has the dreams at first.

"Relax," she'd said. "They can't tell you your future."

But I wasn't convinced. Alone at night without a shield to ward off the nightmares, the fear of drinking sank its teeth deep into my neck and I worried: Was I fighting a losing battle?

The relapser at the podium opened her pitch by saying: "I'm glad I know now I have a committee in my head that's out to get me." Tears gleamed in her eyes and her face crumpled. Someone walked forward and handed her a tissue. She took a few moments to get hold of herself.

Some people called alcoholism's run-amuck, booby-hatch thinking "The Committee." I'd named mine "The Twelve Monkeys." The monkeys were a treacherous lot. Always chattering. Always up to no good. Since this morning's catastrophe, they'd slipped out of their cage and I couldn't catch them. They'd been nattering at me so much that I'd smoked more than half a pack of cigarettes already, wishing I could shut them up. Right now, they were determined that I would pay attention to them and only them, so they'd turned their shrill voices up to fever pitch. Five of them stepped forward.

The first one screamed: *You should have known better!*

You quit that job at Minority AIDS Project to lose this one at a half-ass college downtown? The second roared.

Where was your brain? The third yelled

The fact that I'd had my doubts going in for the job interview only made me feel worse now. It had been plain, at the time, that this was one of those johnny-jump-up business colleges that usually don't last. I'd brushed my doubts aside though, thinking I was being paranoid. Twenty-seven years of drinking had effectively stamped out my confidence in my own judgment. Now, I was paying the price for not listening to my instincts.

You're stupid, Frankie, I berated myself.

Stupid, stupid, stupid! Repeated the fourth monkey.

Couldn't you see that student was hell bent on getting you fired? Why did you let her take your job? Screeched the fifth one.

I sighed. From the start, that student had wanted to take over. Wanted to show the class she was running things. She found out I wasn't going to let her when she and I had some minor showdowns. Then, she trumped me by running to the college dean with her eyes full of tears and a story about how I picked on her. The dean—not wanting to lose the dollars the student would take with her if she dropped out—opted to side with the student. Without warning or discussion, this morning, the dean had handed me a pink slip and the one week's pay I had coming. Shame and anger had seeped into my belly as I rose to my feet in her office. Panic had clawed into my back as I'd rushed out to my car.

Those feelings had made me want the bottle. Really bad. And I still did. Remembering now stoked the wanting. Put a high flame under what was already simmering. What was I gonna do for a job?

Have a drink, suggested another monkey in a civilized tone. *A martini lunch would do you good, you know.* Its tone of voice was quite rational. *Can't you just see it?*

Indeed, I could. A long-stemmed, frosted glass. Green olives floating in crystal-clear liquor. I licked my dry lips, remembering the stinging, saltiness of gin and vermouth on my tongue. It would cool the bonfire in my brain that the monkeys had set.

I shook myself away from those thoughts and concentrated on the relapser. She had recovered herself. "What I have to remember," she was saying, "is not to listen to The Committee." Her somber eyes told a story full of grief.

What made her give up? I asked myself. Something big, I was sure. Illness. Somebody died. *Or maybe,* I shivered, *she got fired, like I did.*

The reality of losing my job reared up like a one-eyed giant then. Fired. No job. Unemployed. What was I going to do for money? I didn't have anything saved. Fear unthawed inside me, and a chunk of it rolled down into my chest. *Am I gonna go out, like she did, and get my butt shot full of arrows because I got fired?* The question made me want to run. Run to mother scotch, like I always did when the going got tough. But I had to hang on because you weren't supposed to drink. No matter what. That's what they said. You weren't supposed to drink. No matter what. *So why did she?* I wondered.

As if she'd been reading my mind, she said to us, "I guess you're want to know what it was that sent me out."

The silent room waited. I waited, stiff with anxiety.

"Nothing," she declared in a flat tone of voice.

I frowned at her. What did she mean, nothing? The newcomers in the seats to my left, squirmed. Behind me, I could hear someone strike a match. Some mother's little kid belched. Confused, thinking I misheard her, I leaned forward. The room leaned with me.

Her expression screamed defiance for a moment; then, it changed into something else. Regret? Disappointment? Anguish? "What I mean is," she continued, "I never really thought I was a alcoholic, like you people. And The Committee in my head kept on me, kept saying why not have a drink?"

Yeah. Why not? Two of my monkeys echoed in utter sincerity.

"I ain't had a good reason to go out that door; just didn't think I had a good reason not to." She stopped and looked us over. I could tell by the woman's eyes that she was remembering something. "The Committee asked me 'Why not have one?' and I just picked up. Wasn't nothing in particular sent me out." Her voice broke on the last.

Shockwaves rolled over me. *Nothing? Nothing sent her out?*

We told you, all this A.A. stuff ain't about nothing! Yelled the monkeys, delighted. *We told you so!*

Like a tidal wave, hopelessness crashed down on my head. Then it swept me up like a tsunami and shook me like rags. *Christ, what was the use?* I asked myself. *If nothing in particular could take you out, what was the use in beating my head against the wall? What was the use in struggling every, single day?*

Tears gathered in my throat while the monkeys sang like maniacs: *What's the use? What's the use? What's the use?*

Before I knew it, I was on my feet, and heading in the direction of the coffee pot at the back of the room. Defeat seeped into my heart like the spill of sewer water. *Nothing,* she had said. *Nothing took her out.* I couldn't get my head around it! At the counter, I stuck my cup under the coffee pot spigot. Hot, black liquid spilled out into my cup.

Why should I keep hanging on by my fingernails? I fumed resentfully. *Why?*

A headache decided to skirt around the back of my skull as I thought about the thirty dollars in my bank account, and the three hundred dollar paycheck in my purse. My four-hundred-fifty-dollar rent was due in three days. What the hell was I gonna do? How was I gonna pay my rent?

Maybe you should just let go of the whole thing, said one of my monkeys.

Go ahead, throw in the towel. Who could blame you? Sympathized another.

In response to that I heard my sponsor's voice in my head, saying: "We don't drink, no matter what."

I smiled to myself bitterly. Well, at least, I would have a good excuse for going out. Not like that relapser woman. When they asked me why, I wouldn't be saying it was nothing that took *me* out.

Leonard ambled up to the counter and gave me a smile.

I glared at him. *This is too hard!* I wanted to scream at him, scream and then run out and find a martini.

Why not go get one? The monkeys sang. *Why not? Why not? Why not?*

Like the relapser, I realized, at that moment, that I had no answer. None at all. Suddenly, my feet began to move, heading for the door.

"Take off your running shoes and stay a while," said a new voice from the podium. It was Sam.

I stopped, frozen, in my tracks and peeked back over my shoulder. Leonard, who was spooning a ton of sugar into his cup, checked me out, grinned again, and gave me a thumbs-up sign. Though I wasn't feeling it, I acknowledged his support with a weak smile. It was the best I could manage.

"Don't leave five minutes before the miracle," Sam said.

People in A.A. had a million slogans, a litany of code talk for every crazy impulse you had, for every half-baked idea you came up with, for each and every misery you thought you'd die of. This was a new one I hadn't heard before. It intrigued me in spite of myself and I backed up.

"If you think you've got a reason to drink," Sam said, "think again."

He definitely got my attention with that one. I decided to go back to my chair.

The monkeys didn't like that. Their jabber had pushed me toward the door. I wasn't supposed to come back and sit down. But they weren't going to give up. They chanted at me like a tone deaf choir. *No-job-no-money. No-job-no-money. No-job-no-money. What're-you-gonna-do-what're-you-gonna-do-what're-you-gonna-doooooo?*

In counterpoint, Sam said: "You can find a lot of excuses to take one. Money worries for one."

As I sat down, I looked at Sam, mystified. How did he know? That was a real mystery to me, how the old timers always seemed to know what was going on in your head.

Sam looked at me and said: "But we don't have to drink, even if we want to." With twenty-two years in, Sam, who always wore his salt and pepper hair in a ponytail, had a load of wisdom and experience to offer. I listened to him because he came from the heart.

"Everything is a test, you know. Whatever the problem is, this, too, will pass." He paused, his eyes shifting from me to the other newcomers in the front row. "Stuff happens. It's called life. We used to try to find relief from it in a bottle. But I'm here to tell you, you can get relief from problems by talking about them. Talk to your sponsor. Talk to other A.A. people. Raise your hand and come to the podium."

The monkeys clamored for my attention. Screaming like mad things, they were doing their best to turn my insides into a boiling volcano. *You really screwed up! Really, really screwed up!*

I ground my teeth and wrenched my attention away from the sound of their voices. I wanted to hear what Sam was saying.

"There is a tremendous amount of hope in these rooms. It's where I found mine," he said. "This program is an inside job. Just like a caterpillar changes inside its cocoon, we change inside when we work this program. Do the footwork and the change will come, I guarantee you. One day you'll look up and the obsession will be gone. You'll be free."

Free, I said to myself, feeling something warm spread its soft wings into my chest. Butterflies—blue, white, purple, orange, and gold—rose in a glorious cloud before my eyes.

"Hang on. Stay with us and remember: We don't drink. No matter what because it's the first one that gets us drunk. One is one too many."

"And a thousand ain't enough," a male voice hollered out, finishing the well-known saying.

As Sam left the podium, the room rumbled with laughter, acknowledging the pure truth of that declaration.

Inside my head, the monkeys yammered: *How you gonna pay your rent? How? How?*

Finally fed up, I knew it was time for me to turn the tables on the monkeys. No more skirmishes with them like this one if I could help it. When the monkeys saw what I intended, they fought and kicked frantically, but I reached out anyway, grabbed them by their scruffy necks, slapped them into their cage, and turned the lock. For good measure, I dropped a blanket over them to muffle their screaming voices. The last thing I heard was: *How you gonna pay....?*

I didn't know how the rent would get paid, but I knew one thing. I wasn't gonna drink. Not today. Not tomorrow either, God willing. I wasn't gonna drink, one day at a time. What's more, it was time for me to do some things to make sure of it. After taking a deep breath, I looked at the leader and, for the first time ever, I raised my hand. The leader pointed to me.

I stood. "I'm Frankie and I'm an alcoholic," I said, then walked, without hesitation, straight to the podium.

Roger

1. Shadow of Death

I looked into Roger's eyes and saw that he was going to die. That thought filled me with a well of tears that threatened, any second, to spill over and drown us. Drown Roger, me, drown Lauren and Mike who were standing beside me at the foot of Roger's bed at Chris Brownley Hospice. He lay unmoving on his back, his arms, small as twigs, folded atop the sheet covering him.

You'd think with me working at Minority AIDS Project for the last two years that I'd be used to it by now, used to seeing AIDS come round, lay its scabby, ruinous hands on folk and then slowly and with great care lay them waste. But I wasn't. Nobody was. You didn't, you couldn't get used to it. And some days you wondered just how long you could take it, looking on as people you'd grown to admire and love fought to live as the virus sucked them in like quicksand. Every day. Until it took them under.

Tears stood visibly in my eyes, and by concentrating all of my will, I held on to them. Just barely. All three of us were struggling not to fall apart. Which was why we'd come together during lunch to help each other hold the fort. And there was another reason. One we couldn't bear to say aloud. Coming together was better because none of us wanted to be alone when we saw what we didn't want to see: That pale horse on the horizon, its rider galloping steadily on, coming to gather another, a beloved, into its bony arms.

Nobody spoke. We hadn't seen Roger for three weeks, not since that last time at church; what we were witnessing had, momentarily, paralyzed us, wiped our minds clean and rendered us mute. Mike's cocoa-smooth face looked mottled, as if someone had punched him in the stomach. Even Lauren, ordinarily unruffled and calm, looked shaken. Casting about frantically for something to say, I opened my mouth and closed it several times before I could speak.

"Roger," I finally said. It was obvious that Roger was too weak to talk and I stood there, anxiously wringing my hands. He looked over at me, trying to focus, trying to smile. "Lindsay and I are getting married in September. We expect you to be there with Darrell, you know." As soon as the words were out of my mouth, I felt like an idiot. What was I thinking? This was June. My wedding was a lifetime away for Roger. Wondering why I had I started this, I stumbled on. "So, so you've got to rally and get home in time for it."

We were all floundering, trying to find something to hang a thread of conversation on. Mike glanced about and I followed his line of sight, really noticing the room for the first time. Cards of every color, flowers, and teddy bears were everywhere. A huge, bright banner with inky, well-wishing messages from Unity Fellowship Church hung from the ceiling. I'd signed it myself two weeks ago.

"I'm going to brush your hair, Roger," Lauren said into the silence. "Would you like that?" Her voice was soft and soothing, like a cat purring.

It took some effort on his part—turning his head, dragging his eyes slowly, very slowly to her face—but he managed it and gave her a nod. Lauren picked up the brush from the little table beside his bed. The paint of her long fingernails, red as blood drops, caught and held my eye as she stroked his hair in smooth, even movements. Before, Roger's hair had been a thicket of soft, tight, little curls that would have resisted the pull of the brush; now the hair was sheer threads of wavy silk, lying close against his scalp and the brush seemed to glide over the hairs on his head.

My eyes slipped down from Roger's hair to his coffee skin. It lay on his bones as dusty-dry as the leaves of fall. Even his skull seemed to have shrunk and the pillow behind his head billowed like an enormous white sail. The look of him sent shockwaves through my brain. I blinked, hoping that blinking would clear away this scene, somehow make it all instantly disappear like Jeannie used to do in that old television series. But nothing changed. I was still standing there staring at Roger. Who was dying, after all.

Thoughts scrambled in my head. Was it just seven months ago, at the Halloween party he and his lover, Darrell, had thrown, that I'd watched him hugging people, dancing every dance, laughing loud and hard at somebody's joke? Was it just seven months ago that I'd been sure he would beat this thing and live forever?

But how could he not? For the two years I'd know him, he'd looked so good that the heads of both women and men swiveled to follow him when he walked by. I'd seen it firsthand when Roger volunteered to go with me as one of MAP's HIV Prevention speakers. I'd watch people's eyes squint in disbelief or their expressions melt into dismay when he told them he had the virus. I'd been there when they looked him over, their eyes slowly caressing the bulging muscles of his arms or the sculpted chest, molded from hours of hard work at the gym.

"You'd never guess," they'd say, almost licking their lips as their eyes moved down to his slender waist, his flat stomach, and the cupcake roundness of his butt.

"Not him. He looks so...so healthy," they'd say, their confused brains, trying to match the vision of Roger's young, handsome, smiling face and his athlete's body with the revelation that he was carrying HIV.

Yes, I could understand why they didn't believe it. He didn't look sick. Not then. But now, now, the disease had plundered and pillaged his body like an invader taking the spoils of war. It had shriveled him like a dried out melon; it had shrunk him down to a shell of himself as if all the water had run out of his body. It had made him an old man in the blink of an eye.

The enormity of the ravage staggered me.

Lauren, serene as the Madonna, still quietly brushed. My mind, shocked and jumbled, did a topsy-turvy flip, drifted away, and down-spiraled.

Roger's not the only one sick and dying, said the voice inside my head. *What about the others you know?*

I counted them, the ones that I knew. My neighbor, Ronald; James, the photographer; Poncie, who was in the choir; Gerald, who was going to be in our wedding; Steve, Charles, Robert, George, and.... Others lined up in my mind. I could see their faces there, but, suddenly, they wavered; my windpipe closed up and I couldn't breathe. Couldn't bear to count. Was I going to have to see them all waste away? Was anybody going to be left? In my head, a line of flower-banked caskets stretched away, receding into the distant, empty horizon.

Each Sunday, there'd be somebody new showing up at Unity: Men whose skin was now the color of ashes; men whose skin had been bronze, red-boned, high-yella, panther-black; men whittled down to no bigger than a minute by the knife of the virus; men coming, sick and hanging on by their fingertips, coming with canes to help them walk, coming clutching pillows to cushion their sore, frail bottoms. Men coming. Looking for sanctuary. Waiting for a touch. Needing to be loved. Not judged. Loved. Not shunned.

My head reeled under the assault of my own thoughts. At some point, Mike had opened his mouth and a stream of words fell out. Something or another about work. It didn't matter what he said. The words were a bulwark for us. Something to hang sanity on. While he chattered, I noticed that Roger's eyes had that look that the dying get—remote, glimpsing a thing, or a place, or a time that our eyes can't see. I wished I hadn't caught that look in Roger's eyes. It bumped hard against hurt spots inside me, still unhealed, that I didn't want to mess with. It reminded me of seeing that look for the first time in my beloved Uncle Madison's eyes as he lay in the hospital, dying of cancer. It reminded me of seeing it in Daddy's eyes, ten years ago. Seeing it and understanding that he'd caught a glimmer of the landing across the water and wanted to go. I hated knowing that he wanted to go, wanted to let cancer and alcohol float him across Jordan on board that old ship of Zion. I hated it because I didn't want him to go.

I shifted my eyes away from Roger's. After Daddy, and because he was the last of my blood family, I'd thought I was through with all this. For a while, at least. Through with having to go through hospital corridors that smelled of stale sheets and piss and rot. Through with seeing disease reduce people to frail and faltering shadows of themselves.

The last time I'd seen Mama was in a room like this one. Pain rippled behind my eyes at that memory. After all these years, the claws of guilt still tore into me when I thought of her. The beginning for her had been losing her breast.

"Don't worry, Frankie," she'd assured me on the phone, in 1962, after the operation. "It's all over now."

But it turned out that it wasn't. Three years after, I could see that she was getting weaker though I'd never really believed, couldn't believe that cancer would get her, like it did Grandmama. Couldn't believe it because I didn't know of anyway to get ready for that. That Thanksgiving weekend of 1965, with Mama lying in that hospital bed, I could see things I hadn't wanted to see before. That her hair, always shining black, was now very white at the edges. That her face, always bright and alive, was now haggard and pale as smoke. I could see things in her eyes that I hadn't seen before either. Things telling me what I didn't want to hear. The worse part was that I didn't have the guts to face it, say things that I should've said, do things that I should've done. At her bedside, I saw her eyes slide away, more often than not, to gaze beyond, out into a distance further than time and deeper than space. And I felt, in the depths of my heart, that she was poised at the edge, that I wouldn't be able to hold her back. That, in the end, I would have to give her up to Death. Forever.

And here I was again. At a hospital, at a place where Death hung around like a hungry hyena.

You thought you were safe for a while, but Death came and found you. Said the voice that lived inside my head. *Now what are you going to do?*

It was as if I'd come full circle in a nightmare from which there was no escape. The landscape of Death was different this time—uncharted, unmapped. But it was Death all the same. What was I doing here?

Shaken, I gripped the railing at the foot of the hospital bed while a pool of unspent tears, somewhere deep inside, strained slowly into my lungs; they were turning into a cry, into a shriek that was crawling up my throat. I turned my back and walked toward a window, struggling to catch the shriek and stuff it down. I squeezed my hands together as if to crush, once and for all, the thick overflow of feelings welling up in my chest; without warning, anger suddenly surged forward and crowded out all else. Its fierceness stung me and I raged silently.

This virus had robbed us of a passage of time in our lives that ought to have been free of fears about a fatal disease, free of Death. Age, that brought close the stink of the grave, was still in the distance. Why was this happening to us?

I turned back. For just a moment, the room and the people—Roger, Lauren, and Mike—seemed frozen in time, outlined in a strange starkness that chilled my heart. As I looked at Roger's face, puckered with age come too soon, the anger boiled away, evaporated into grief. We were far too young for the shadow of Death to be at our shoulders. Far too young to be burdened with this weight. But, young or not, Death was here anyway. I could see his pale outline standing there beside Roger's head.

2. 5149 West Jefferson

He died a week later. His memorial was the Saturday following in the Minority AIDS Project building. Just before his service, I stood at the door leading into the big room that served as Unity's sanctuary on Sundays and for memorials. In a daze, I stared at one of the MAP-Unity posters tacked to the hallway door. It pictured Roger, Steve, and Reverend Bean, all of them smiling broadly at the camera. Rev, dressed in his white pulpit robe, had his hands on their shoulders. I gazed at Roger for a long time, wells of sadness filling me up, remembering that last time at the hospice.

A tear broke away and coursed down my cheek.

No blubbering today, Frankie, I told myself. *Tears are a luxury you can't afford.*

But tears aren't a luxury when you need to grieve, are they? Said my voice.

I ignored it, too afraid to think about that. I was already wrestling with questions that I'd been lugging around: How long could I keep on being around dead men walking? At church on Sundays and at work everyday. How long?

It had dawned on me the other day that I had been spending a good deal of my life in 5149 Jefferson for the last two years. I was here at least six days a week. Sometimes, seven if something was going on, like a meeting, or a training session. Or a memorial. With that realization, a worrisome question had popped up that begged for an answer: What in the world was I doing working at a place where we looked into the jaws of Death everyday?

I was the one who ran from things for most of her life. Running from college down the road a piece to hide out in Evansville, Indiana for thirteen years, drinking everyday, passing for straight, scared to live my life. Running in place and going nowhere until a double dose of Death rousted me out of my hidey-hole and ran me clear across country to Los Angeles.

Yeah and a good run is better than a bad stand, right, Frankie? Said my voice.

Damn straight, I agreed.

So how did you run yourself up in here? It asked.

I had no answer to that, but I thought about it. Here I was working at a place where desperate, frightened people came in every day. People always in need, people despised for crossing borders or sneered at for not fitting in; people held cheap for being poor, and banished for the sickness inside them. Sometimes, working here made me feel like that mythical king, Sisyphus. The one condemned to forever push that huge rock up a steep, mountain incline to the crest, only to have it roll back down every time, forcing him to start pushing all over again. In doing HIV Prevention, I had to deal with all those things that spread the virus as much as blood and cum: The sexual attractions all tangled up with shame and self-hate; the self-sacrifice, poverty, and oppression tied into being a woman; the greed for power that fed racism; and the homophobia that bloomed everywhere like lilies of the field. Like that king, soon as I'd roll that damn rock up to the top and leave it there, I'd turn around to see the thing rushing back down the mountain ready to mow me down. Jesus! What was I doing at a place where everyday was a fight to get money from the city, the county, the state, the feds—from bureaucrats and politicians that guarded it, but didn't want to give it up to help people survive? A place where it was always a fight to just to keep enough food in the pantry for people who came in needing a package of dried beans, a can of fruit, some meat and bread. People who came in with eyes telling us they needed much more than food. Needed things like hope. A hug. And a bit of love. If we could spare it.

Noises from the back hall jerked me out of my reverie. I sighed, put my hand on the doorknob, and turned as the big, red letters at the top of the Roger-Rev-and-Steve poster stared up at me: *Love is for Everyone,* the words said. A load of gnawing feelings that I didn't want to deal with dropped into my stomach as I went inside the sanctuary.

Somebody had placed a large vase of pink, yellow and purple gladiolas on the table up front. In the corner near the pulpit, the choir had taken their seats, waiting for their musical cue from Darren, the Music Director. The room was nearly filled with people sitting quietly in the gray, metal, fold-up chairs that had been carefully lined up in neat rows by church volunteers. There was no bier, no coffin, and this was not a traditional funeral. It was a memorial. A remembrance. A home-going celebration. But I didn't feel like celebrating. No sir. Not one little bit.

The beige, paneled walls that I knew so well now seemed a bit too close for comfort. Silently fighting the urge to run out, go somewhere else, anywhere else, I sank into an end row seat near the front and saved the one next to me for Lindsay. As I sat there, listening to Darren play a hymn softly on the piano, Reverend Bean and Reverend Zach, both robed in white, walked into the pulpit while Darrell, Roger's lover, entered, escorted by the ushers, Christine and Ana. They seated him in the front row, just as Lindsay hurried in and took the seat beside me. She took a look at my face and squeezed my hand.

I scanned the room. Looked at the brown, black, and yellow faces. The men, young, mostly in their twenties, looked strained, heart-heavy, and careworn. The women, somber, dispirited, pensive. There were no signs on our chests, but we were the scapegoats. They'd stamped us misfits, labeled us depraved, branded us an abomination—all because we were born same sex attracted, or both sex attracted, or trapped in bodies of the wrong gender. And with the advent of this disease, we had been cast out into the wilderness and left there. As what? A sacrifice? An appeasement? An offering? No one cared that we would die. They were all afraid. The preachers had turned their backs. The doctors had slammed their doors. And so here we were, an ancient clan trudging this wasteland, blistered, bone weary, and alone.

Darren's fingers touched the keys, signaling the first song from the choir. They rose, and a tenor voice offered encouragement. *They, that wait on the Lord,* the voice told us in slow measures and with great tenderness, *shall be renewed in strength....*

I looked at Reverend Zach. He sat with his bronze hands gripping the arms of the pulpit chair, his young, lean face transfixed as if he had discovered some great treasure hidden within the music.

The lead singer went on in a voice that was full with tears and hope. As he sang, I recognized this song as a verse from the book of Isaiah. He was the prophet, I remembered, that told the Hebrews if you had patience and if you put your hope and trust in God, things would turn out all right in the end. The song went on while I silently mused about that. I had my doubts. Where was the end anyway? This road we were walking ran off so far into the distance that you couldn't even see the end. I looked from Reverend Zach to Reverend Bean whose walnut-brown face was in repose, his head nodding in time with each piano chord. He'd started it, this walk we were on. He was leading us. What could he see? Did he know where we were going, where we'd end up?

Anguish settled over me like a heavy veil. Just what, in God's name, were any of us doing at MAP, taking on Death as our adversary in a battle that surely we were going to lose? What good was it doing? We were dying anyway. A tiny little virus had hurled us, blind and lost— God help us—into the mouth of the wilderness, into an endless desert, into a fearsome, unknown country without compass or canteen. How were we going to survive it? Death was taking us down in double-quick time. And I didn't want to be here watching at the end. It was going to be too painful.

Teach me, Lord, how to wait, the choir sung in perfect harmony, responding to the lead singer's call.

Wait? My head responded. *Wait? Uh-huh. No. I have to get out of here. Wait for what? You can't outwait Death. It comes out the winner every time.*

I'd fooled myself into believing I'd made peace with it. But I hadn't. Death was the Gorgon. Medusa. The Reaper. The sum of all fears. And I didn't want any part of it. Not again.

Though I was struggling to keep them at bay, memories took a scalpel and sliced into my brain, exposing wounds still alive, still pulsing with grief. I was four years old and back at East Vine Methodist Church, screaming while Mama was taking me away from Grandmama, rigid and unmoving, in the casket. I was twenty-one years old, dry-eyed and swaying in agony, as I leaned over Mama's rose-covered casket, hoisted above the freshly dug grave. I was thirty-six years old, standing in an Evansville mortuary, one April morning, looking down at Jay, silenced once and for all by a bullet that tore into his neck. Two months later, I was trembling in a Knoxville mortuary, looking down at Daddy—whose sweet Hershey bar face had become a grotesque Death mask, barely recognizable to me.

Now, the choir had swung into the song in full measure. *Be of good courage,* they sang. *Wait on the Lord,* they said. And before I knew what was happening, something had come undone inside me. Like rocks breaking free of a mountainside, there were tears. Tears, suddenly, here on my face. Embarrassed, I wiped at them with the back of my hand, trying to stop them before someone saw me. But they kept coming. And coming. Without warning, they had become a cascade.

Lindsay put her arm around me and Ana brought me tissues from a Kleenex box. Why couldn't I stop? The tears bewildered me Where were they coming from? The harder I tried to stop them, the more I could feel things breaking apart inside me. Breaking apart and rolling downhill becoming a rockslide. Tears loosening the load that I was carrying, had been carrying for so many years. The guilt, the fears, and the doubts binding me were giving way under the gentle assault of tears. They felt like mountain rain on a hot summer afternoon. Tears, like a balm. Soothing. Mending. Restoring. I couldn't stop them, couldn't fight them. So I gave in and let them do their work.

At the end of it, we went outside, standing in clumps and pairs, there in MAP's parking lot, waiting for Reverend Bean to finish it, finish the memorial by giving us words to let go of Roger, so he could be on his way. We'd replaced the tradition of going to the cemetery to see someone's body put into the ground with the ritual of the balloon release. A rainbow bouquet of balloons symbolized the spirit of the one who had died; releasing the balloons into the sky signified the journey homeward. Christine and Ana came round handing out balloons to everyone. I took a red one. Lindsay took green. As soon as everyone had a balloon, the final litany began.

Above us, I watched clouds, looking like pearls that someone had scattered, floating lazily on a backdrop of ocean-blue; it was bright and clear and warm, instead of the usual, June-gloom, gray day. Before I knew it, the balloons were going up, rising heavenward. Their upward flight reminded me of an old spiritual and I hummed it under my breath, silently reciting the words.

We are climbing Jacob's ladder. We are climbing Jacob's ladder. We are climbing Jacob's ladder. Soldiers of the cross. At the end of the stanza, I finally let go of my red balloon and watched it—watched Roger—make his way, riding up and up into the deep and endless sky. Going home.

After the benediction, Lindsay drifted away to talk to someone. But I still watched the red balloon on the tail end of the others, all of them disappearing, one by one, into the soft blanket of blue. Paul, my colleague at MAP, came over and stood beside me, smoking quietly for a few moments. We both watched until they'd all gone.

"See you Monday for the 8:30 meeting, Frankie, right?" He asked.

I looked at him, and opened my mouth to say: *No*. To say: *I've had enough and I'm not coming back to MAP and all this death*. I'm sure that's what I was going to say.

But what I said was: "Yeah, I'll be here, Paul. Bright and early."

Pandora's Box

1. Coffee and Advice

When I told Pete, over coffee and rolls, that I was going to come out to the people back home, the force of his voice carried loud and clear above the Saturday morning sounds at the Farmer's Market .

"Are you insane?" He shouted at me from across the table. "Don't do it!"

Startled, I almost jumped out of my skin. As it was, I splashed some coffee on my pants. At the next table over, some well-to-do-looking White people turned and looked at him. Pete ducked his head apologetically at them. They gave him a blank stare for a moment before going back to their conversation.

Disapproval put a deep scowl on his nut-brown face. "Who in the world gave you that bad advice?" He asked, voice noticeably lower. The clatter of dishes and the traffic outside on Fairfax had me straining to hear him this time.

"Umm, nobody, really," I said, feeling and sounding a bit timid. His response had knocked me back a peg.

"Nobody? Well, why in the world would you, then?" Pete picked up his cup. His pinky finger stuck out in imitation of dainty delicacy.

"Because," I said, "I can't be getting married and be in the closet, Pete!"

He looked at me like I'd gone soft in the head. "Telling people is in such awful taste, dear, don't you know that?"

"I don't think honesty is in bad taste, Pete."

"But everybody will—will know," Pete sputtered, outraged at the thought, He paused and shifted gears. "You'd be cutting your own throat, Frankie."

I said nothing to that. I was still trying to recover my balance from his initial response. I'd been looking for support, not censorship. Or, at the least, understanding. Instead, I felt like a child being scolded. Maybe because Pete always sounded like a proper school marm.

I'd met him before I started working at Minority AIDS Project, at a time when we both were teaching at one of the quadrillion business colleges dotting the landscape of Los Angeles. I was teaching Proofreading, which was more English grammar than anything, and he taught Sociology, but he had Hollywood dreams of going into fashion design.

"It's working at that place, isn't it?" His tone was accusatory. "I told you not to do it," he reminded me, smug and self-satisfied.

Why had I brought this up? How could I have forgotten that, two years ago, it was Pete who'd admonished me not to work for Minority AIDS Project?

"It'll ruin your career," he'd said when I called to tell him I'd gotten a job there. "People will think you're...."

I'd finished his sentence."A Lesbian? Queer? Gay?"

"Well, quite frankly, yes!" He'd sounded appalled. The conversation had gone downhill from there. After that, we hadn't talked for months.

Pete's glasses slipped down and he pushed them back into place. "Being around all those people has just ruined you," he lamented.

I stared at Pete. Short, just this side of plump, Pete was Gay and closeted and under the impression nobody knew simply because he worked hard to make sure nobody would guess. But however hard he tried, his slip was still showing, so to speak. The way he drank coffee or tea, holding the little finger of his hand out delicately; that was a very queenie thing to do. Straight men didn't do stuff like that. And, apparently, there were other things about him that people could clock him on. I remembered the time while we were still teaching together when one of his students had come to me, bitching about the grade she'd gotten in his class. After she'd finished venting, she'd told me that Mr. Holden—Pete—wasn't fooling anybody with his act. She'd said she knew that he was Little Richard's sister. I'd had to work hard to keep a straight face behind that.

Because he'd have been mortified, I'd never told Pete what that student had said although, at the moment, the thought was crossing my mind. *All those people?* If I hadn't just come from an eight o'clock A.A. meeting, I would've cussed him for the nasty, little queen he was. But recovery made you think twice before you did things. So I lit a cigarette and held my tongue. But I took revenge by deliberately blowing smoke in his face.

While he coughed daintily from the smoke I'd blown in his vicinity, I repeated: "All those people?" There was a dangerous edge in my voice.

"You know what I mean. Gays and Lesbians going around identifying themselves to the world! Some people don't have sense enough to keep their business to themselves," he declared, adding sugar to his coffee. "I mean, why draw attention to yourself? What's wrong with blending in? Isn't that what this country is about?" He was on his high horse and feeling really good about it.

I sipped my coffee silently. Blending? I'd had enough of that—of being a cheap imitation of straight people. Enough of forcing myself to walk their walk. It was the same as being chained in a slave coffle. And quiet as it's kept, blending took your freedom. It made you a slave. You just didn't want to see it that way.

Pete mistakenly took my closed mouth to mean he could take some liberties. "And that church you go to, some kind of cult, I heard. People say..."

"Wh-hoa! Stop right there! I'm a second away from cussin yo ass out!" I'd had enough. I wasn't going to let him diss Unity. Not by a long shot.

He closed his mouth and waited for me to cool off. Without speaking, we watched the parade of Saturday morning shoppers. They looked like they were from the neighborhood: Mostly elderly and White, along with some Hollywood industry types who drifted by, toting coffee or juice and sweet rolls.

Finally, he broke the silence. "Frankie, why open up Pandora's box?" Pete asked, genuinely mystified. "Telling people can stir up such terrible feelings. Why invite trouble?"

That was true enough. Still, there was another side to the argument. "What about my feelings?"

He shook his head. "They don't matter."

"Why not? I've been stuffing them for years, Pete. Till it hurts. And you're telling me they don't matter? Why not?"

"Here's why," he said, pushing his eyeglasses up to the bridge of his nose the way he always did before a class lecture. "Like it or not, you have to recognize that, generally speaking, people don't much like us different ones."

It was the first time I'd ever heard Pete identify as Gay, however oblique. And that sent a mild shock through me. Where was he going with this?

Pete stared into his open palms as though he were telling his own fortune. "Conformity drives the herd instinct and it demands that everybody be the same.

Sameness presents no threats, you see; the herd remains safe." He paused and looked up at me suddenly. "Difference, however, makes waves which will rock the boat. And, dear, when the boat rocks, people become nervous and afraid."

"So I have to keep pretending so they won't be nervous and afraid?"

Pete picked up his coffee, tasted it, made a face, and put it back down. "Yes, you do. Because when they're afraid, they get nasty. And nastiness turns very ugly, very quickly."

"That's crazy. We're talking about people I've known all my life. Not some wild mob." I stubbed my cigarette out and anxiously lit another. What he was saying brought out my anxieties because his line of reasoning was exactly why I'd stayed in the closet all these years.

Pete sighed. "You never know how they're going to react until you open your mouth and tell them. You don't know whether they'll be friend or foe. As for family and friends, they can be nastier than a mob and uglier than Frankenstein. Take my word for it, I know."

I was taken aback, and deeply distressed at his words. My brain was working furiously to refute what he'd said, only I couldn't come up with anything.

He dabbed at his moustache with a napkin and stood. "Want more coffee? I'm getting a refill."

"Sure." I watched him go, feeling frustrated and disheartened.

At one of the market stalls, I could see customers bending over tomatoes, picking and choosing, dropping them in the brown bags that the vendors provided. Outside, car horns blared and beeped in the thick of traffic on Fairfax. I sat thinking about Pete's attitude, his advice. It had put a gray misery over my heart. I'd wanted bolstering up, not a bunch of reasons to make me change my mind. I puffed on my cigarette, completely at bay and thoroughly shaken now.

Pete put our coffees down and then sat. "Why risk it? What do you hope to gain by it? Telling people, I mean."

"The truth," I said, picking my coffee up. There was a touch of self-righteousness in my tone, and I gave myself a mental slap on the wrist for it. Self-righteousness was a nasty piece of business. Not a good thing for me to indulge in. Still, I wanted to get back at him for tearing into my carefully-built threads of confidence about what I was going to do.

"And what does truth buy you, dear?" He asked sarcastically.

"No more hiding," I said, promptly. "Which buys me my life."

"Does it? Do you think the truth will make you free?"

I blinked at him, confused and drained of confidence by his questions. "Won't it?" I asked. And added feebly, "It's supposed to."

With pity in his eyes, Pete gave me his answer. "Frankie," he said, "that's only in fairy tales."

2. High Stakes

The phone sat on my desk like a green toad. I wanted to pick it up and dial Knoxville, but I was scared to. Pete's warnings, a couple of hours ago, had set up the worse kind of doubts in my head now that I was home.

When I finally reached for the phone, a voice from The Corners said: *What will you say if somebody asks you to explain Jay being your lover?*

I pulled my hand back and thought about that. About what people nowadays would call my sexual identity and how I'd played tricks with it. Worn false colors. Hoodwinked everybody. Years of tricks and trickery.

How was I going to explain myself? Would I say I wasn't heterosexual though I'd masqueraded as one? Would I say I wasn't bisexual though given my sexual history, some might try to label me that way? I'd woven quite a convincing illusion. So convincing that, now, even I had to wonder about some things.

And what does the truth buy you, dear? Pete had asked.

Some relief, I hope, I answered while my thoughts catapulted back in time.

Why had I crossed over to men? First and foremost, because of what had happened with Stacey. She'd been my first lover, male or female, and she'd been my Waterloo.

I'd fared no better with the next woman. Two strikes and it seemed to me that I was out. *What's wrong with me?* I'd asked myself after the second strike and, as if I'd summoned ghosts from the past, a scene materialized: Auntie and I stood facing each other in the old Mee Street kitchen.

"Nobody wants a sassy girl like you," she said, glaring at me with her wolfie eyes. "Why, why would anybody want a girl like you," she looked me and up and down, her lips curling back in a sneer. "Nobody wants you," she said, turning her back.

Why would anybody want you? Her voice repeated in my brain, echoing down through the corridors of time: *Nobody wants you. Nobody wants you. Nobody wants you.* Like a tape stuck in a loop, for years, her words circled round in my brain. And I believed them. Wholeheartedly.

If nobody wanted me, I'd thought, shame crawling through me like a lava flow, *if I don't appeal to women, then, I'll cross over. I'll settle for men,* I'd reasoned, trying to salvage my sense of self-worth that had somehow gotten mortally wounded years ago. Life would be easier that way anyhow, I'd thought. All I had to do was bury my woman dreams in secret corners and forget about them. And that's the way it had started with men. I'd crossed in Evansville and then, Jay had come along.

I went into the kitchen and pulled out the instant. I hated instant, but coffee had become my constant companion these years that I'd been in A. A. I'd managed to burn up the coffee pot a few days ago, so I had to do instant today. The stove's gas jet whooshed into flame and I carefully lit a cigarette from it before I put a pan of water on to boil. How would I ever be able to explain all this stuff? I stared out the kitchen window at the lemon trees, smoking and thinking back. Jay. Truth be told, our relationship had been built on lots of liquor, good sex, and no risk for marriage. From time to time, when Jay had to attend to hearth and home, I'd distract myself by doing a one-night-stand with another man though Jay had been the one I'd claimed to love.

But how, asked the voice from The Corners, *could you have loved him if you've always been a Lesbian?*

The water boiled and I poured it over the instant. Coffee cup in hand, I went back to sit at the desk across from the phone. Had I convinced myself that I loved him to distract me from being who I was afraid to be? That was a disturbing question and I took a couple of long, hard pulls on my cigarette to soothe the disturbance. Before I could speculate on that one, my brain sent another memory swooping down to rattle my cage. Had I simply used Jay as a dam to hold back the flood of my desires? And when the dam was gone—well, it was embarrassing to remember that less than six months after he'd been dead, I'd slept with a woman. And how in the hell had that happened? My woman dreams were supposed to have been long dead and well buried. How could the desires have come back? Grief over Jay alone should've kept them away. But it hadn't. And women had become the lodestar of my universe again. As if Jay had been only an interlude.

I put out my cigarette. *Stop,* I told myself. *You can't really explain all this to yourself, so how do you think you'll ever be able to explain any of it to anybody else? Just pray nobody asks.*

I looked at the phone sitting there curled up like a green viper.

Who in the world gave you the bad advice to come out? Pete's voice echoed in my head.

I did, I answered. But did I have the nerve to do it? With a stomach full of butterflies, I got up, backed away from the phone, and went to the bedroom to change into my gardening clothes. Gardening was something that I'd taken up to fill the void. To take the place of mother scotch. To keep the twelve monkeys gagged, so I couldn't hear any of their wacko suggestions. Especially when I was agitated. Like now.

I stepped outside. The August afternoon shimmered blue and California hot. From my porch, turning to face north, you could see the tops of palm trees neatly laid out in rows, running all the way back to the hills and mountains beyond. The "Hollywood" sign rose on the horizon like an icon from my dreams. Somewhere, in a parallel universe, it was Saturday afternoon in Knoxville, Tennessee and ten year-old me was crossing Vine Avenue at the stop light, walking up to the Gem Theater's booth, paying my ten cents, and entering the eye of Hollywood's magic lantern. Knoxville. Home. Was I going to have to give it up? Would I have to if I told them?

Why risk it? Pete's voice asked me.

This was high stakes, I knew. It was a risk to put my cards on the table. To bet everything. If I lost, I'd lose Knoxville, the place I was born, the place where I grew up, the people I loved. The whole enterprise scared me shitless. Risks scared me shitless. Because I'd been programmed never to take them.

For some reason, I stood there remembering the movie, *Indiana Jones and the Last Crusade,* remembering the risk Indiana took to save his father. Standing at the edge of a gorge, he had peered down at nothing, except a chasm, miles deep. If he turned and went back, his father would die. If he went forward, if he stepped out, it looked as if he'd be taking a fatal plunge into the deep.

I walked around to the side of the house and got the shovel. I could hear dogs barking in the distance. As I came back into the front yard, I asked myself what was worse? Taking a chance and stepping over the edge of the gorge, like Indiana, or turning back because I was afraid? His foot had hit solid rock when he'd stepped over. There'd been a bridge there all along. He just couldn't see it. If I stepped out, would there be one for me?

I went back into the front to weed around the white, long-stemmed hybrid roses bordering the stepping stones that led from the street to the porch. As I neared them, a waft of their sweet scent touched my nose. I stuck my nose into the center of a rose and savored it for a moment. On the street, little kids were running up and down the sidewalks, screaming as they chased a rubber ball. Memories of Mee Street, of me, Evelyne, and Shirley playing at The Square, memories of Knoxville flowed into my head. I stuck the shovel into the ground to loosen the dirt around the roses. Who was I going to tell first?

Telling people is in such awful taste, dear. Why cut your own throat? Pete's words kept circling in my head.

In Knoxville, the short list was Aunt Avice, Judy, Brenda, Janice and her husband, Calvin. Janice was the first friend that I could remember having. We were in Nursery School together. And in Austin High's band together. I remembered us—the tiny tot mascots—marching behind the Drum Majorette, lifting our little legs high to the beat of the band's drum.

Smiling, I wondered: Where had time gone? Wasn't it just a few years ago that I was having my annual, junior high school sleepover parties with a dozen squealing, clowning girls? Girls all over the living room, eating popcorn and hotdogs, listening to Ruth Brown and LaVerne Baker. Janice was at most of them until she went away to school. Later, when I'd had the last one in high school, Brenda was there and Nancy and Judy and four or five others. More memory pictures spilled out of my mind and I was seeing me at Y-Teen Camp, along with Brenda, Janice, Nikki, and Nancy. I could see us swimming, hiking, and watching a star-filled, night sky as we sung around a campfire. Those were good memories. Ones that pressed on the heart strings. I stopped shoveling, for a moment, and memory's lens clicked one final time. I could see us in cap and gown at our high school graduation, lined up to march down the aisle, nervous because we knew we were about to scatter to the four corners without any idea of where we'd end up. I looked up at the Hollywood sign. Where had it gotten to, the time? In my mind's eye, I could see it, running on ahead, an invisible, flowing river, taking us on a raft to parts unknown.

I sighed and shoveled up a chunk of dirt. As I did, I saw I'd caught a worm. It wiggled desperately to get away from the light and back into the bosom of the earth.

Why draw attention to yourself? What's wrong with blending in? Pete's voice asked.

I bent down to pull out some weeds, watching the worm wiggle-waggle away as the aroma of green grass and roses drifted past my nose.

Soon, the heat of the day pressed in on me. Dropping the shovel at the foot of the porch steps, I decided to go inside for something to drink. In the kitchen, I opened the refrigerator door. On the top shelf sat a quart of Sunny

Day orange juice. I stared at it, remembering the orange juice queen, Anita Bryant and her notorious media campaign. Watching her on T.V. that day at Allen's came back in full force as fragmented voices rose and fell in my head. They sounded like a radio signal almost out of broadcast range.

We have to stop these homosexuals!

Lock em all up!

What they're doing is immoral and goes against God's wishes!

They freaks of nature, man!

Tears stung my eyes. Is that what my friends back home would call me if I told them? A freak?

Pete's voice cut in. *Telling people can stir up such awful feelings, dear. Why ask for trouble?*

I took out a bottle of water and shut the refrigerator. *Maybe telling would be a mistake. Maybe I should listen to Pete.*

Aunt Avice's smiling face framed by a cloud of short-cropped, white hair, appeared in my mind. She was Uncle Frank's second wife and my only living relative. When Daddy died, ten years ago, his second wife had insisted we all go to the mortuary together to see Daddy's body. I hadn't wanted to because I wasn't good at that. At seeing somebody I loved wrapped in death's embrace. My knees had turned to jelly when we'd gone in. And then the shakes had started. Hard and uncontrollable. I'd felt like I was going to fly apart. When Aunt Avice saw me shaking, she'd gathered me in her arms and held me tight. Since Daddy's death, we'd been very close and I treasured that. What would she think about me if she knew? Would telling cut me off from her? I didn't know. And not knowing felt the same as running out of air under water.

Back outside, I sat on the porch steps. The sun was hot and high in the sky. I wiped a droplet of sweat from my nose and drank some water, thinking about the people in Knoxville. The ones that I'd grown up with, gone to high school with. What would they say? Would telling mean I'd have to give them up? And could I?

Pete's words came back once more. *But why open up Pandora's box?*

He'd been referring to a Greek myth, an old story with two different endings. The ending you'd favor depended on your perspective about life. In one, Pandora opens the box and all the human ills of the world fly out; in the other, Pandora opens the box and all human blessings fly out, leaving only hope inside. It was obvious which one Pete favored. The question was: Which did I buy into?

Left with my own runaway imagination, I could depend upon the twelve monkeys in my head to cook up fantasies of disaster at the first sign of a problem. Given my alcoholic thinking, I was prone see the worst possible scenario just around the corner. But I'd learned by listening in A. A. that what actually comes down the pike never matches up with the disaster scenarios we make up in our heads.

Since I had concluded long ago that I was no Cassandra—that I really couldn't see around corners, now what? Was I gonna let the monkeys win out and scare me away from doing the right thing? Or was I gonna do an Indiana Jones and take the risk?

I stood up, opened the screen door, and headed for the phone. My hands shook as I reached for it. I hated this feeling. It was like the one I'd had at Y-Teen camp so many years ago as I was standing at the edge of the diving board, trying to get my nerve up to try my first dive. Anxiety had rippled up and down my stomach as I stared down into the water nudged into tiny waves by the afternoon's gentle breeze. A tightness had circled and clinched my chest. The others had done it—glided to the end of the board, bounced up once, and dived, arching their bodies to neatly cut into the water. Now, it was my turn, but I was scared. Scared of doing a belly buster. Scared of people laughing at me. Scared of God knows what. Just like right now.

I looked at the phone again. The day in Allen's when Anita Bryant had said those awful, lying things on T.V., I didn't have the guts to speak up and tell them who I really was. Belonging, fitting in with the group was the most important thing to me, then. But now, here I was getting ready to kiss belonging and fitting in goodbye if need be.

What had happened since then?

Time. An ole tune rolled through my head and I could hear Sam Cooke's velvet-smooth voice singing: *It's been a long, long time comin, but I know, I know change is gonna come.* What had happened? Time bringing things to my doorstep that had changed me. Like working at Minority AIDS Project. Like going into Alcoholics Anonymous, and like finding Unity Fellowship Church. Change had come on time's coattails. A.A. had birthed it in me and Unity was breast-feeding it. As for MAP, well, Pete had been right about Miss MAP changing me, but wrong about it ruining me. Working at Miss MAP gave me backbone. And courage. I wasn't the same woman now as I was that day in Allen's.

Reverend Bean's voice spoke softly in my ear: *You are not a mistake. You are God's creation, made in the image and likeness of The Creator. So, love yourself.*

Since I wasn't a mistake, why should I keep on living like I was? Acting like I was? I had to admit, it was scary, this idea of stripping off my camouflage. I thought about Henry, Jewel's bartender, living exposed, in his own "glorious personae as a queen." How would it feel to live in the world like that without camouflage? I didn't know, couldn't imagine. What I did know was that camouflage did something to you. Something toxic. Something deadly. If I let it, it would kill me, one day. Kill me deader than a doornail. And I wanted to live. That's what had really changed about me. I wanted to live.

I dialed Aunt Avice. While the phone rang, I realized I was holding my breath.

Breathe, I told myself. *Breathe. In. Out. In. Out.* My stomach twitched like a cat's tail.

"Hello," Aunt Avice said.

"It's Frankie, Aunt Avice, how are you?"

"Well, I'm fine now that I'm talkin to you, darlin." Her southern accent was as sweet as maple syrup.

"Aunt Avice," I said, standing, like Indiana Jones, at the edge of the gorge, "I have something I need to tell you about me."

And as I stepped off the edge, I saw hope rising, like a butterfly, from Pandora's box, then, felt, suddenly, the blessed assurance of something solid beneath my foot.